How the Coa...

Split (1825) into Eastern (Kent) Division controlled from Deal and Western (Sussex). Division controlled from Newhaven. A chain of Semaphore Signal Stations was set up in 1820 viz:

North Foreland

THE DOWNS

South Foreland

IRS

① Deal

② Easthill

③ Little Cornhill

④ Hougham Court

⑤ Martello tower No. 4

⑥ Fort Moncrief

⑦ Martello tower No. 27

⑧ Battery No. 2

⑨ Dungeness

⑩ Jury's Gap

⑪ Martello tower No. 31

⑫ Fairlight

⑬ Galley Hill

⑭ Kewhurst

⑮ Martello tower No. 55

⑯ East Langley Fort

⑰ Beachy Head

DUNKERQUE

GRAVELINES

CALAIS

BOULOGNE

FLOGGING
JOEY'S WARRIORS

FLOGGING
JOEY'S WARRIORS

How the Royal Navy fought the Kent and Sussex smugglers

John Douch

"I really begin to think they mean to shoot me in earnest"
(Capt W. McCulloch RN, written report to the Admiralty,
from HMS *Ganymede* lying off Deal, 10th February, 1817.)

Crabwell Publications/Buckland Publications Ltd.
2 The Ridgeway, River, Dover.

To
Walter Jameson McCulloch, MC, TD
of
Ardwall, Kirkcudbrightshire

The author is pleased to state that a share of the proceeds of this book will be given to the BRITISH SAILORS' SOCIETY.

Published jointly by Crabwell Publications and Buckland Publications Ltd.

ISBN 0 906124 08 5

Printed in England by Buckland Press Ltd., Barwick Road, Dover and 125 High Holborn, London WC1

CONTENTS

Illustrations	7
Bibliography and sources	9
Prologue	11
With Peace Comes War	13
The Terrible Trade	22
Before the Blockade	27
Hurrah for the Life of a Sailor!	31
The Hierarchy	43
The People at Work	46
A Third-rater	51
The Coast Blockade	60
Early Days	61
A Hard Man?	66
McCulloch Makes his Mark	69
The Struggle for Supremacy	79
Expansion leads to Escalation	83
Baiting the Blockade	85
The Purser and the Pea-shooter	89
Some Clerical Criticism Contained	93
'A Hard Fighter, of Reckless Courage'	94

The Coast Blockade (Continued)

The Brookland Affray	89
Hastings defies the Blockade	93
The Tragedy of Sydenham Snow	94
The End of the North Kents	104
Hamilton's Ordeal	105
Murder by the Bathing Machines	107
More Mayhem at Hythe	109
Spreading the Net	110
The Trap is Sprung . . .	111
. . . but the Gallows are Cheated	113
Stood Down — Paid Off	114

Appendices

(a) The Men	118
(b) The Ships	132
(c) Some Naval Terminology	137
(d) McCulloch's Record of Service	145
(e) McCulloch's Family Background	146
(f) The Report of a Royal Commission	150
(g) The Blockade in Fiction	154

ILLUSTRATIONS

How the Coast Blockade developed	End Papers (front)
Early SE Coast Guard stations	End Papers (back)
'The Minute Gun at Sea'	10
Anchors etc.	12
A Volunteer Force	14
Dover, too, had its day	16
'Concealments'	19
Dover from the sea	24
Tools of the Preventiveman's Trade	25
Rye from the ferry	26
A Riding Officer	29
New Bethlem Hospital	32
A Sailor being flogged	34
A Midshipman of the Blockade	36
A Frigate	38
The Naval Hospital, Greenwich	40
Dover Castle	42
The Naval General Service Medal	45
A Boatswain, RN	46
HMS *Wellington* off Dover	52
The main compartments of a '74'	54
Figureheads of a '74'	56
The stern of a '74'	58
The lower-deck of a '74'	59
St Leonard's Church, Deal	62
The Port Admiral's Residence, Deal	63
Barholm House	64

No-man's Land, Margate 70
In the Downs 71
The Naval Hospital, Deal 72
A Martello Tower after artillery practice (1891) 74
Broadstairs Cliffs 76
Plan of a Martello Tower 77
The Timeball Tower, Deal 78
Sandgate Castle 80
Sandgate from the sea 81
The Blockade's Budget 82
Deal from the sea 84
The cracked window 92
A Smuggler's Church 96
Fairlight Glen 98
Hastings — Fishermen's Quarters 100
Smugglers and Fishermen 102
The Press Gang 102
The Ship Inn, Herne Bay 103
Scene of Morgan's Murder 106
Announcement in the *Kentish Gazette* 106
The Casemates today 108
The Bourne Tap 110
McCulloch's signature 116
Boarding the Chesapeake 117
The *Captain Digby* inn sign 119
St Mary's Churchyard, Walmer 120
St Michael's, Newhaven 123
The *Walnut Tree Inn*, Aldington 128
A prison ship 131
HM sloop *Enchantress* 134
A brig of war 138
Warship ratings 142
A Captain's Letter 144
Cardoness Castle 147
William McCulloch's memorial tablet 147
The Arms of McCulloch of Barholm 148
Landing goods at Bo-Peep, Hastings 149
A Coast Blockade Station 159
Launch of a Deal Lugger 160
Halt — Smugglers 161
Jack's Farewell 162

Bibliography and Main Sources

Admiralty Papers—a selection at the Public Record Office.
Boteler J. *Recollections*. 1910.
Carson E. *The Ancient and Rightful Customs*. 1972.
Chatterton E. K. *King's Cutters and Smugglers*. 1912.
Colledge J. J. *Ships of the Royal Navy*. 1969.
Customs Commissioners, The *Twelfth Report to the Treasury*. 1821.
Douch J. A. *Smuggling, The Wicked Trade*. 1980.
   Rough Rude Men. 1985.
Finn R. *The Kent Coast Blockade*. 1971.
Gardner J. A. *Recollections*. 1906.
Gentleman's Magazine—various volumes. 1816-31.
Gill C. S. (ed) *The Old Wooden Walls*. 1930.
Glascock W. N. *A Naval Sketch Book* (1st series). 1832.
Glover N. *Nelson's Rotten Navy* (article) *Military History* May. 1983.
Gordon L. L. (rev. Joslin E. C.) *British Battles and Medals*. 1971.
Henderson J. *Sloops and Brigs*. 1972.
Laker J. *A History of Deal*. 1917.
Lewis M. *The Navy of Britain*. 1948.
   A Social History of the Navy 1793-1815. 1960.
Marshall J. *Royal Naval Biography*. 1823.
Masefield J. *Sea Life in Nelson's Time*. 1905.
O'Byrne W. *A Naval Biographical Dictionary*. 1849.
Scarlett B. *Shipminder*. 1971.
Shore H. (later Lord Teignmouth)
   The True History of the Aldington Smugglers.
   (Series of articles in the *Kentish Express* 1902-03).
Smith G. *Something to Declare*. 1980.
Sutcliffe S. *Martello Towers*. 1972.
Teignmouth, Lord and Harper C. G. *The Smugglers*. 1923.
Walls A. J. *A Pictorial History of the Royal Navy*. 1970.
Webb W. *Coastguard!* 1976.
Williams N. *Contraband Cargoes*. 1969.
Wilson G. *Old Telegraphs*. 1976.

Personal communications
W. L. Birch, J. Colthup, L. W. Cozens, J. F. Fone, E. Green, W. Lapthorne, P. Manning, P. Muskett, W. J. McCulloch, E. Stage, C. Waterman, E. Weston.

THE MINUTE GUN AT SEA,

Duet,

IN

"UP ALL NIGHT"

OR

The Smuggler's Cave,

Composed by

M. P. KING.

...Sta.Hall.

Price 1/6

LONDON,

THOMAS BROOME MUSIC SELLER & PUBLISHER, 15, HOLBORN BARS, E.C.

Smuggling was a very popular theme for the early 19th century dramatist and song-writer (see Rough Rude Men). *One likes to think that even 'Flogging Joey' himself would have spared a sardonic smile at this song's titles.*

Prologue

*Never before, in a time of profound peace, were
Naval officers called on to perform more invidious
duties; history, naval or civil, may be searched in
vain for even an allusion to the Force. . .*

This was the situation some sixty years ago as described by
Lord Teignmouth, one-time Commander in Queen Victoria's
Navy and latterly Inspector of Her Majesty's Coastguard.
Today, it appears little changed; apart from Lord
Teignmouth's own work (see Bibliography), books dealing
with Customs, Coastguards, smugglers and the like make only
passing reference to the Coast Blockade. For some reason,
Captain William McCulloch RN, its founder, remains
shrouded in obscurity; of the seventeen sources I consulted for
information about him, only two succeeded in getting his
Christian name, the spelling of his surname, his naval rank
and the year of his death all correct. Even Lord Teignmouth
fails on the last point and a modern naval academic in an
article dealing specifically with smuggling at that period gets
his Christian name wrong — and promotes him to Admiral!
There is, however, one notable exception; the thirty
fascinating pages of Ralph Finn's *The Kent Coast Blockade*
which fired my imagination and steered me towards a deeper
investigation of that unknown, unsung, unhonoured band
which, however much maligned, however much neglected,
laid an undeniable part of the foundation upon which our
modern Coastguard Service stands.

As material for this book accumulated, I was to find myself

11

becoming increasingly intrigued by the character of Captain William McCulloch RN. Often depicted as a flogging enthusiast of the old school, sometimes described as a sadistic monster, was he, perhaps more credibly, simply a hard man doing a difficult task to the best of his undoubted ability? What of those who served under him? What were their backgrounds, how were they trained, how did they face up to the Wicked Traders? What happened to them when the Force eventually disbanded? With three thousand possibilities to investigate, the field was wide, not to say confusing, and yet it is my sincere hope that with the resources at my command I have produced an account of which Lord Teignmouth would have approved and which, even at this late hour, may still stand as a small memorial to those of the Royal Navy who, in the course of an arduous, highly unpopular and, some might say, a not very heroic duty, served, suffered and died, often alone and always outnumbered, at the hands of fellow countrymen, here at home on the shores of Old England.

Anchors, etc. (E. W. Cooke, 1828)

With Peace Comes War

*Wherever there is water to float a ship, we are sure
to find you in the way!*

Napoleon's remark addressed, of course, to the Royal Navy,
immediately lost all its previous significance with France's
final subjugation. With Nelson's work at Trafalgar completed
some ten years later by Wellington at Waterloo, peace,
retrenchment and reform soon became the order of the day.
Smuggling soared to heights hitherto undreamed of and the
ranks of the 'free-traders' swelled daily with a massive influx of
discharged servicemen, skilled and drilled in the art of war
and still hopefully seeking profitable adventure. The Royal
Navy, although drastically curtailed by peace, was still very
much a force to be reckoned with and was now in a position to
pay these would-be entrepreneurs far more attention than had
been possible in the past years of the French wars.

Cuts in the Royal Navy—Ships in commission 1814/1820

	1814	1820
Ships of the Line	99	14
Ships not of the Line	505	92

NB A parallel reduction in man-power also occurred; from a
peak of 145,000 in 1812, it dropped in three years to 90,000
and by 1817 had plummeted to below 20,000.

The early 19th century was a period of political turmoil,
economic uncertainty and social change; this is an obvious fact

and yet it must be emphasised if the truly national importance of smuggling be not overlooked. The dream of legal Free Trade still lay fifty years ahead; meanwhile, the levies upon those items which the ordinary citizen was gradually coming to regard as necessities of life—tea, tobacco and spirits, not to mention the luxuries of lace and silk (of which, it is recorded, one 'high-class London store' alone illegally acquired some £200,000 worth annually)—were certainly high enough to justify the considerable risk to liberty, limb and even to life itself which involvement with the sharp end of the Wicked Trade entailed. On the land, the farm labourer was the system's humble backbone; more often than not with a large and growing family to be provided for, such a man seldom needed little persuasion to supplement a meagre income with

A volunteer force similar to the Home Guard of 1940. (see page 15)

a modicum of night work now and then shifting contraband bales and kegs for the 'midnight men' — work which in a few hours would bring him as much the same number of days honest mundane graft on the land. He, the 'land-smuggler', was, not without some justification, regarded by the farmers and local gentry with a certain suspicion. The year 1803 saw the French poised yet again to invade our shore. Lord Sheffield, the Lord Lieutenant of the Northern Division of the Rape of Pevensey, wrote to his superior, the Lord Lieutenant of Sussex (the Duke of Richmond), outlining his defence plans for his district. It seems that 'persons of property' had already come forward with suggestions that a volunteer force, similar to the Home Guard of 1940, should be raised:

'If the Legion should ever assemble, I suggest that the Skirmishers, which is to be formed from Ashdown Forest and of Smugglers, Poachers (whom it may be necessary thus to occupy that they may not take a worse course), and unsightly men (with whom the Farmers would not choose to rank) should be on the left . . . This is the largest and wildest Division of the County, there is a bad breed of Smugglers, Poachers, Foresters and Farmers' Servants who, in the case of confusion, are more to be dreaded than the March of a French Army. . . (*A History of the Volunteer Forces,* Cecil Sebag-Montefiore 1908, quoted by J. R. Williams in *North Pevensey Volunteers of the Napoleonic Wars* see *Sussex Family Historian* Vol. 6 No. 2 June 1984).

The man who actually brought the goods over from France was a totally different breed. These "sea-smugglers" were usually excellent seamen and were highly sought after by the Royal Navy within whose ranks they were required to serve five years if caught in their nefarious pursuits. Not only the British navy but Napoleon himself held them in great esteem and allowed them an astonishing latitude for they were the main source of his intelligence: 'During the late wars, all the information I received came from the (English) smugglers.' He allocated them a special enclave in Dunkerque where they could come and go as they pleased, but 'They latterly went out of their limits, committed riots and insulted everybody. . . ' This Cup-Final behaviour obviously could not be tolerated; the smugglers were quickly transferred to Gravelines where they could find less scope for mischief. Here were to be found

DOVER REGATTA BALL,

Patronized by the Right Honourable the Countess of Liverpool and Mrs. Jenkinson.

THERE will be a BALL at the ASSEMBLY ROOMS, Dover, on the Evening of the Regatta, THURSDAY, 7th September, 1826.

Dancing to commence precisely at Nine o'Clock.

Captain GALE,
S. K. JARVIS, esq.
S. M. LATHAM, esq.
E. P. THOMPSON, esq.
} Stewards.

Admission Tickets, Gentlemen, Six Shillings—Ladies, Four Shillings.—To be had at the Libraries and Assembly Rooms. Dover.

DOVER REGATTA.

PATRON:

The RIGHT HON. THE EARL OF LIVERPOOL.

VICE-PATRON:

R. H. JENKINSON, ESQ.

BOAT RACES AND SAILING MATCHES IN DOVER BAY,

On THURSDAY, the 7th Sept. 1826, at One o'clock.

FIRST RACE.

By FOUR, Four-oared 28 feet, DOVER GALLIES.

SECOND RACE.

By FIVE, Four-oared 28 feet, DOVER GALLIES.

A SAILING MATCH to take place between the Races, should the weather be favourable, by Four Sailing Dover Gallies.

THIRD RACE.

Between a DOVER, Six-oared 32 feet, GALLEY, built for that purpose, and a FOLKESTONE, Six-oared 32 feet GALLEY, for a SWEEPSTAKES of FIFTEEN SOVEREIGNS, to be rowed and steered for, by Boatmen of the respective places.

This will be a very interesting trial of skill between the Boatmen and Boat Builders of two of the most celebrated Towns on the Coast, and in which it is expected the Boatmen of Deal will join, they having been challenged to enter the List.

Previous to the Races there will be a procession of Boats round the Flag Stations.

The Committee of Management in acknowledging the liberal Subscription already received, venture at the same time to hope that it may yet be increased, and that the Public, amidst the pleasures and amusements of the Day, may feel that they have been the means of rewarding and encouraging a very useful and necessary class of Seamen, whose intrepidity and humanity, stand most conspicuous, in the promptitude of their Assistance to Crews of Ships in Distress or Wrecked, even at the risk of their own Lives and Property.

Dover, Aug. 29, 1826.

** Subscriptions are received at the Banks and Libraries.

Dover too, had its day— three weeks after Deal.

16

the great contraband warehouses, the Napoleonic hyper-markets where the goods could be chosen, packed and paid for in a manner quite reminiscent of today's legitimate practice.

Ironically, at one of the peaks of smuggling activity along the Kent coast, there was a carnival atmosphere in the town of Deal. Scarcely one week after the murder of Morgan (see p. 111) the *Kentish Gazette* (8th August, 1826) announced:

DEAL REGATTA BALL

patronized by COUNTESS VERULAM

Stewards: Captain Pigot RN*, Captain Baker RN, Captain Boys RN, Captain Boteler RN, Lieutenant E. Cannon RN.

Tickets to be had on application to the Stewards, and afterwards paid for at the door. Ladies 4s, Gentlemen 5s (Transferable to Ladies only).

Dancing to commence at Nine.

DEAL AND DOWNS REGATTA

This very interesting trial of skill with MEN whose superiority in managing their well constructed BOATS is universally acknowledged, is fixed for TUESDAY, the 10th instant.

A very commodious and safely erected GALLERY will be placed in front of the THREE KINGS HOTEL, commanding the whole of the course, equally with the Balcony of the Hotel, immediately opposite to which the WINNING POST is situated. Tickets 2s 6d each may be had at the THREE KINGS, No. 18 Middle Street and No. 100 Beach Street, Deal.

Immediately beneath these announcements there appeared the Customs House offer of a reward of £500 to anyone giving information leading to the arrest of the killer of Quartermaster Morgan (see p.106).

In its next issue, the *Gazette* gave good coverage of the regatta and the ball which followed:

'The Port of Deal possessing natural advantages equalling, if not surpassing, those of any place in His Majesty's Dominions, it required merely a hint to the Nobility and Gentry of the neighbourhood of its capability to

* See Appendix A.

create a feeling in its favour which, being improved upon and brought into action by the exertion of a few spirited individuals, eventually produced the exhilarating spectacle witnessed on Thursday last . . . Arrangements were all completed by 8 o'clock at which hour his Majesty's ship Ramillies of 78 (*sic*) guns (by order of her gallant Captain) and the Honourable East India Company's Yachts, and other vessels in the Downs were simultaneously, and as by enchantment, decorated with colours of all description. . . By noon, the town was literally thronged. At 1 o'clock precisely the Boats started for the first race. . . the commencement and termination of each race being announced by signal guns from his Majesty's ship Ramillies.

The rowing in some of the boats was of the most beautiful description, and the exertions of the whole of the men employed in the matches were prodigious. At the conclusion of the races, the prizes, contained in elegant purses decorated with ribbons, were distributed by the Right Hon. the Countess Verulam. . . the Treasurer, Edward Iggulsden, Esq., (*The Mayor of Deal*, see p.73), addressed the boatmen and the public, complimenting the former in her Ladyship's name on their skill and exertions displayed that day and congratulating the country on possessing a body of brave men, devoted as the Deal boatmen are to the duties of their calling, risking as they frequently do their own lives for the preservation of the lives and property which the perils of navigation and the dangerous quicksands, by which they are surrounded, so often place in jeopardy; and expressing her Ladyship's desire to contribute by all the means in her power to the well-being of those brave men and of the town at large. Her Ladyship then, with the grace and condescension which so eminently distinguish her proceeded to deliver to each seaman the prize awarded, accompanying each purse with a few kind observations, evidently affecting the rough but honest tars to whom they were addressed . . . The roughness of the sea prevented many of the passengers from landing from the steam-boats and other pleasure vessels in the Downs but . . . moving masses of well-dressed persons of both sexes paraded the beach; the windows, houses and boats opposite the sea were filled with elegant families, the Stewards' balcony was occupied by the Earl and Countess of Verulam and their lovely family, and by Lord Carrington . . . Admiral Thomas Harvey, Admiral Sir Edward Owen, KCB, Captain Pigot RN, the Worshipful the Mayor &c., a long list of Officers and fashionables of both sexes, every staff and place at which colours could be hoisted being filled with national and other emblems, presenting on the whole a *coup d'oeil* surpassing anything of the kind ever witnessed on this coast before. The festivities of the day were concluded by a most brilliant ball at the assembly rooms. . . music of the first description being brought from London for the occasion. The dancing was kept up with much spirit until a late hour. . . in this manner ended a fete which proved itself deserving the distinguished support it received. . . which we sincerely hope will prove a forerunner to many others of a similar description not only at Deal but at the other ports of Kent. . .'

What were the reasons for this festivity? Was the Establishment (the Royal Navy in particular, perhaps) anxious

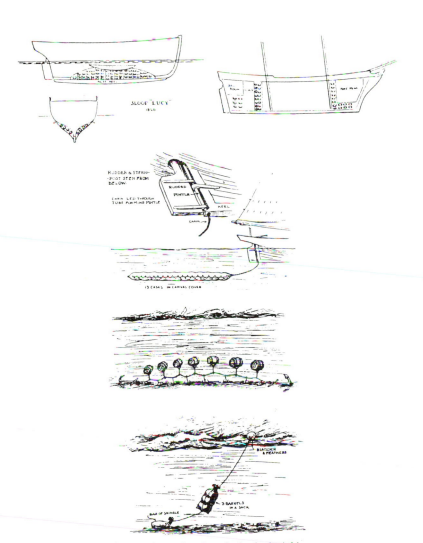

"Concealments" and methods of tub-sinking.

to 'show the flag', demonstrating to all and sundry that it was not to be intimidated by the murderous activities of a handful of ruffians a few miles along the coast in Dover—or was it more a conciliatory gesture by the local gentry towards 'those rough but honest tars' who, comprising the majority of Deal's male population, must have all, in one way or another, been associated with the illicit economy? For many an onlooker, feelings and attitudes may well have been mixed; humane sympathy for Morgan's widow on the one hand being counter-balanced by business interests on the other.

It was of course common knowledge, as we have just seen, that only a few years previously the Kentish smuggler, one foot in each camp firmly astride the Channel, was not only able to carry messages for both sides but was also the medium by which bullion, good golden English guineas, was transported to France and thence down into Spain to pay King George's enemies engaged there in battle with Wellington's Army of the Peninsula. Adding insult to injury, those French prisoners of war who could afford it were regularly spirited away from our shores back to their native land—by courtesy of the Whitstable smugglers. It was indeed, widely held that the Kentish free-traders were at the bottom of the rural unrest which swept the county in 1830; many feared that French revolutionary ideas (they, the French, having just disposed of their monarch for the second time in less than forty years) were permeating into England along with the silks, spirits and tobacco. Whether that was so or not, the smuggler naturally resented and resisted any attempt to interfere with what he saw as a perfectly natural way of life. In diarist Fanny Burney's 'sad smuggling town of Deal' there was a great reaction when the Coast Blockade was 'laid on' in 1816 as Laker in his *A History of Deal* relates:

'All the boats in the Downs were watched and followed; directly they landed, McCulloch's men swarmed down to the beach and searched the boats and persons of the crew. If any contraband goods were found, both men and boats were seized. All this was very galling to the boatman, whose employment was fully confined to attending on ships in the Downs. It angered him to have his boat and his person overhauled as soon as he came ashore; it was contrary to his natural liberty of going afloat and returning when he pleased. Such as pursued the illicit trade set their wits to work and every contrivance that could be hit upon adopted. . .'

Penalties against boatmen caught smuggling were practical and severe; the vessel was destroyed by being cut across into three and the owner heavily fined. Had he offered armed resistance, five years service in the Royal Navy was the least he could expect; other possibilities were transportation to Van Diemen's Land or to Australia (or, in the previous century, to North America), even a public hanging. Until the 19th century, however, the mere possession of contraband was not, in itself, an offence. The history of smuggling may not be particularly honourable but it is undeniably long with roots stretching back to the 13th century when King John instituted a system, basically the same today, with Boards of Administration ('six or seven of the wiser and more learned men of substance, and one clerk') strategically placed at the then major ports. Over the next five centuries, the government was to carry on a running battle with the law evaders who often came off best. Communications across country, where any existed, were very difficult and in any case the army, who might have been able to control illegal importations, was never available in sufficient strength due to other commitments abroad.

At long last, however, the tide seemed on the turn. With Boney safely locked away on St. Helena, the British lion found that, for the time being at least, there were no more foreign enemies left to conquer; he was therefore able to turn his attention to that festering smuggling sore which had given him such trouble for so many years. Other factors soon arose to militate against the Fair Trader; the newly invented macadamised road and the equally new-fangled steam locomotive were on the point of extending their tentacles into the very heart of rural England. Soon, very soon, the fastnesses of the desolate shingle beach, the wind-swept headland and the sunken woodland track, until then known only to their native fauna and to those who followed the secret Trade, would be inviolate no more. But this is to anticipate; before that happened, a mighty struggle was to be witnessed along the coasts of Kent and Sussex.

The Terrible Trade

'They (the Kent smugglers) are a terrible people with the courage and the ability to do anything for money' (Napoleon Bonaparte).

Typifying these 'terrible people' was the Aldington or South Kent gang, also known as the Blues, possibly because of the colour of their working gaberdine smocks. They were based on Aldington village perching high over Romney Marsh upon the escarpment which was once, in prehistoric times, a cliff-top. From this well-nigh impregnable position they came and went much as they pleased throughout the Marsh and ruled the coast from Camber to Deal. Eventually, the Coast Blockade was to prove their undoing but for the first quarter of the century they flourished almost without check. People who knew them personally—fellow villagers and actual gang members—passed on their recollections in old age to Lord Teignmouth who published them in a series of newspaper articles over eighty years ago (see Bibliography). These have proved invaluable in building up a picture of how the smugglers actually conducted their business. George Ransley (1780-1856) was the last, and the best known, leader of the Aldington gang; his full life story is related in *Smuggling—The Wicked Trade*. Born and raised in the district, George, in common with most of his coevals, was a smuggler to his very fingertips, although he did not fully enter the Trade until he married a smuggler's daughter; until then he made his living as a carter on an Aldington farm. Unusually strong, both mentally and physically, he had a

22

cheerful, practical, outgoing nature and was a born leader, besides which he had a natural affinity with horses which must have stood him in good stead when loading the goods and getting them away off the beach. As was the way in those days, once married, he and his wife Elizabeth set to and produced a goodly crop of young ones. The first son, George, has left this account of how their affairs were conducted:

'My father, a farm-hand by trade, took to smuggling first to make money. He used to smuggle tea, tobacco, brandy and sometimes playing cards *(these items first attracted tax in 1709 to help finance the war with France; it was not abolished until 1960)* from France. He would leave by packet from Dover *(whence the first steam vessel left in 1820)* and cross over to buy a boat there that would carry about 200 tubs, each holding 3 ¾ gallons each *(these were the famous 'half-ankers')*. This boat would be manned by sailors got by my father on purpose to bring over the goods; they lived mainly at Folkestone. After buying the goods, he would arrange for them to be brought over to England at a certain time and place; he would employ a certain number of men to be on the look-out for the boat's arrival. Each side of the chosen landing place fifteen men would be posted to keep back the preventive men while the goods were being unloaded; these men were called 'scouts' *(also 'batmen' from their oak cudgels or 'bats' which were carried and used to fearsome effect)*. Besides these about a hundred or more 'tubmen' were on hand to carry the goods away from the boat; they got 7/6 a night for their work and the scouts were paid one guinea apiece. The tubs, costing about £1 each in France, fetched £4 in England but at that time it was impossible to buy a gallon of spirits from an English merchant for less than £2.5.0. The goods were landed at different places along the coast from Rye to Walmer so as to avoid detection; they were sometimes brought across in a lugger towing a boat into which they were loaded as soon as they neared the shore. The lugger would then turn back immediately and return to France. Should anything amiss occur to the shore party, father would fire off a warning rocket and the boat would turn around at once and make its way back to France to await further orders. . . it was not unusual for men to be wounded in encounters with the revenue men *(the official term was an 'affray')* and firearms were freely used on both sides. Father would lead the fighting party to hold off the preventive men, while I was at the rear. After being 'run', the tubs would be taken to different hiding places and stored underground in 'tubholes' dug out of the earth and closed by a wooden cover which could be lifted by a chain and ring when required *(see McCulloch's report p. 71)*. My father often sold as many as a hundred tubs in a week, with people coming from over 30 miles away to carry the goods off on foot, on horseback and in carts; those who lived nearby could earn sixpence a week storing them. Our Magistrate was Sir Edward Knatchbull *(a County MP noted for his sympathy for the plight of the farm labourer, his Jury was rebuked for its leniency to the machine-breakers of 1830. Sir Edward was not without his own problems—see 'John Knatchbull—from Quarterdeck to*

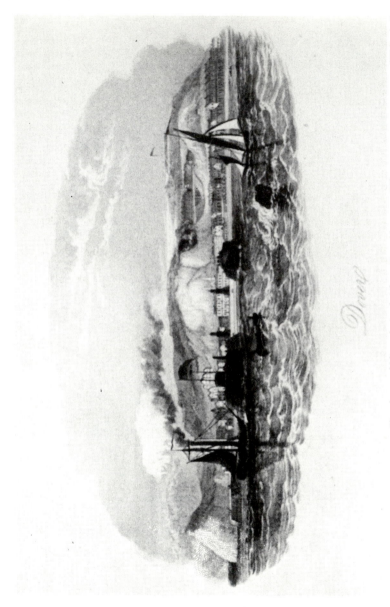

Dover

(Old print)

'Ransley would leave by packet from Dover' (see page 23)

Gallows' C. Roderick 1963); he lived at Mersham Hatch and twice fined father £100 at Ashford for selling spirits from his house *(the Bourne Tap—see p.110)* but the money was never paid. Both those times, he was defended by the lawyers Langham and Platt; once, all his goods were seized and taken to Ashford to be sold on account of the fine not being paid, but they all came home again.

If any man were wounded protecting or carrying the goods, he was always picked up and carried away in a cart to be cared for until he was well again *(see 'Smuggling—The Wicked Trade');* father paid the expenses and if the man had a family, he would see that they were looked after also. The scouts were always armed and often fought the revenue officers. Sometimes carts and horses were lost taking the goods on up to London, seized by the riding officers. Once, when three whale-boats were about to land the goods, a revenue galley with twelve men came upon them, they captured one of our boats with its load. The placed one man aboard her and the rest rowed off to chase our other two, but failed to catch them. Returning to pick up the captured boat, they found it gone; the crew had jumped on the preventive man and pitched him overboard, he was washed up next morning. . . Sometimes when goods were to be landed, the tubs would be fastened to lines and sinkers so that, if the preventive men came up interfering, they could be quietly slipped over the side and grappled up later. . ."

The Tools of the Preventiveman's Trade.

Government issue cutlass, pistol and club; the latter was used also as a probe into 'place of concealment'. (From the Lapthorne Collection)

25

Rye, from the ferry.

(Old print)
(Reproduced by kind permission of Ivan Green)

Before the Blockade

Good days them, when a man might smuggle honest, didn't have to go a-thieving and weren't afraid to die for his principles (remark attributed to an old Deal fisherman).

'The Trade' statistics for 1723-32

Commodity	Seized	Evaded Customs (Estimated)
Brandy	192,515 Gals	2,000,000 Gals
Other spirits	139,104 Gals	1,500,000 Gals
Tea	102,041 lbs	30,000,000 lbs
Tobacco	1,061,248 lbs	20,000,000 lbs

Life was indeed relatively simple for the smuggler in the early days; as we have seen, official interference was perforce limited and, until the Preventive Waterguard was established in 1809, there were but two main obstacles for him to negotiate. First, the revenue cruisers, which, operating far out at sea, were usually evaded with consummate ease, as one of their captains himself had to admit 'It's like sending a cow to chase a hare.' Cruisers, cutters, or sloops (in this context the terms are synonymous) were first employed by the Customs in 1698. Six separate authorities were involved in their control over the British Isles as a whole and it was inevitable that rivalry and friction developed. By 1800, 37 revenue craft patrolled the whole coastline and of these, 13 covered Kent and Sussex. At that time, their activities were viewed with a certain scepticism, at least by the inhabitants of Rye:

'At this place is a custom-house with a very large establishment, a custom-house boat, as it is called, whose crew consists wholly of Landsmen and who, of course, are all freemen. . a cutter is likewise stationed here under the pretence of cruizing against the Smugglers, but in truth by way of giving additional influence to the Treasury. . .this cutter, which is named the *Stag,* is commanded by Captain Wm Haddock who alone has freemen quartered upon him to the amount of £350 per year. However, it is clear that his place will bear this encumbrance as he is rapidly making a fortune. . .'

(Rye British Universal Directory 1798).

Greyhound, 200 tons, was the largest vessel then employed. She carried a crew of 43 and 16 guns and patrolled between Beachy Head and Start Point; smallest was the minute *Bee* with her crew of 9, cruising off the Yorkshire coast. The usual armament was the 9-pounder cannon but the newly invented carronade was becoming increasingly popular.

Having conveyed the goods to the pre-arranged landing place, it was no part of the sea-smuggler's brief to linger for, with the merchandise safely deposited, his part in the contract was fulfilled; from then on it was up to the land-smuggler to get the goods away as quickly as could be. Here the Traders were at their most vulnerable to the attention of the riding officer supported by troops — preferably cavalry — as and when they could be spared, which was never as much or as often as Custom House would have liked.

Romney Marsh saw its first Riding Officers in 1690. The Land Guard, as the newly formed body was called, was charged with the onerous duties of 'preventing the carrying of wool to France *(this, the illegal export of wool, was the earliest form of smuggling and was known as 'owling')* and the bringing over of uncustomed and prohibited goods by the French privateers'. Each Riding Officer was allotted a coastal strip, usually about ten miles long and five deep, which, equipped with sabre and pistols (government issue) he was required to patrol on horseback both by night and day. Often the post was regarded as a sinecure and its obligations discreetly ignored; as the Commissioner for Customs complained in his Report for 1783:

'Apothecaries, Brewers and other Tradesmen who never ride but when their own occupations require it. . . many of them are Agents and Collectors for Smugglers. . .'

Having said this, it should also be pointed out that many Riding Officers died doing their duty; it was a hard life and their wives and families often had to endure unpopularity if not physical violence.

A Riding Officer.

One of a series of pen and ink sketches by the military artist R. A. Simkin made, it is thought, to illustrate a magic lantern lecture given by his friend Dr T. A. Bowes of Herne Bay about a hundred years ago. It depicts Riding Officer Gill, a leading character from 'The Smuggler's Leap' (one of the *Ingoldsby Legends* by R. H. Barham) leading a troop of revenue men out to get Gill's deadly enemy Smuggler Bill. The story is founded upon fact; in the background appears Herne Church where Sydenham Snow is buried (see page 94).

(Reproduced by kind permission of the Herne Bay Records Society)

At times, the army was called upon to assist the Revenue. Dragoons and Lancers, being more mobile, were obviously preferred but the men did not like the job:

'They do not go cheerfully about their duty, as they know their share *(of the reward offered for the capture of contraband)* will be negligible,'

as one officer noted. General Henry Hawley went further than this, he was downright disgusted at the way his soldiers were treated by the rascally revenue men down in Sussex:

'If our men do manage to make a seizure, the revenue officer warns them that by the time their Colonel has cheated them their share will be negligible; after a few drinks he has managed to buy the poor private's share for a pittance.'

An act passed in 1803 empowered the army to seize suspect goods and ships on its own initiative, but by 1830 use of the military had practically died out, although even today they are still required to assist the Revenue when called upon.

Additional to these forces, the Custom House at every main port, headed by the Collector with his staff of Land and Tide Waiters, was often required to confront the free-trader.

With the dawn of the new century, it became daily more obvious that something had to be done. The ever-widening, increasingly expensive gap between the Waterguard revenue cruisers and the Landguard Riding Officers had, by hook or by crook, to be plugged. So it was that in 1809 the Preventive Waterguard was first deployed. It was an amphibious 'in-shore' force mainly nocturnal in habit, as the orders stated:

'As night is the time when the smugglers generally run their cargoes, it is expected that the boat, or her crew, or the greater part of them, will be out, either afloat or on land, as often as circumstances will permit, which must be at least five times a week. . .'

Collusion with the enemy was often suspected, especially by such as Captain McCulloch who regarded the Preventive Waterguard as nothing but 'indisciplined, inefficient and frequently in league with the smugglers' — but then, as the leader of a rival organisation, he can hardly be regarded as unbiased. These then were the forces facing the smuggler before the Blockade got under way; they are described in greater detail in *Rough Rude Men*.

Hurrah for the Life of a Sailor!

(Victorian popular song)

The happiest hours a sailor sees
Is when he's down
At an inland town
With his Nancy on his knees, Yo Ho!
(W. S. Gilbert 1836-1911, *The Mikado*.)

Before further pursuing the fortunes of Captain McCulloch and his men, a digression has to be made to examine the general pattern of life in the Royal Navy of his day, because only by appreciating — in broad outline at least — the structure, traditions and routine of that incredible institution can one hope to arrive at reasonable understanding of how the Coast Blockade was formed and how it functioned. Despite drastic pruning in 1815 (see p.13), the Royal Navy was still highly respected across the face of the globe, but for all that, for every minute of their existence afloat, both men and officers (excepting, possibly, the Captain on a large ship) lived and worked under conditions most would now regard as intolerable, conditions which, coupled with the iron discipline and the incredibly cramped living space, plus the daily issue of 'grog' containing the equivalent of half a pint of neat rum, must have all surely contributed to the established fact that more than one in 1,000 sailors were designated 'madmen' compared with the national figure of one in 7,000. An Admiralty asylum was built at Moorfields, London to accommodate these unfortunates. First named the Royal Bethlehem Hospital it was soon widely known as Bedlam and today, some would say ironically, it houses the Imperial War Museum. Sir Gilbert Blane, top naval physician of the day,

31

New Bethlem Hospital, St. George's Fields. (Old print)

advanced a theory to account for the sailor's proneness to mental disturbance. He maintained that the constant repeated cracking of heads against low beams accidentally encountered on board ship brought about a chronic inflammation of the coverings of the brain, a meningitis in fact. These injuries passed unnoted at the time they were sustained as the victims were usually drunk.

Many sailors did indeed suffer considerable physical discomfort, disability even, and yet they contrived to carry on serving. Putting aside the extra stress and danger of actual battle and considering merely the daily routine, the guns (a 32 pounder weighed 3 tons) to be kept ready for action, the heavy canvas sails which doubled their normal considerable weight when wet and yet still having to be hauled in by the topmen (see p.47) lying over the yards a hundred feet or more above a rolling deck, the water and provision casks, the powder kegs, the cast-iron shot; all these to be manhandled and stored away in the hold below; no wonder that between 1808 and 1813 it was estimated that at least 10% of our sailors were ruptured—in that period alone, 25,000 trusses were issued. Apart from the enemy there were numerous other hazards to be faced: tuberculosis, typhus, scurvy and rheumatism to name but four, along with the less likely risks of death by fire, foundering, wreck or explosion. Far at the bottom of the list came the chance of being killed in action or dying subsequently of wounds. Small wonder, perhaps, that the 'seaman went merrily into battle with his mind on prize-money, his eye on the enemy, and his hand on the gun'.

Fatal Casualties in the Royal Navy (1810).

Cause	Number	%
Disease	*2,592*	*50.00*
Individual accident (usually when drunk)	*1,630*	*31.50*
Foundering, Wreck, Fire or Explosion	*530*	*10.20*
Killed in Action	*281*	*5.40*
Died subsequently of Wounds	*150*	*2.90*
Total	*5,183*	*100.00*

33

Cruikshank: A sailor being flogged in 1825.

'They hung me up by my two thumbs
And they slashed me 'til the blood did run
They cut a net 'crosst me back and bum
O! Aboard of the man o' war!'

(Sea shanty circa 1815 included in Stan Hugill's *Shanties & Sailors' Songs 1969*)

What of the dreaded discipline? The basis of Naval Law then, as now, was the thirty-nine Articles of War, laid down in Cromwell's time. Thirteen of them carried the mandatory death penalty if transgressed and thirteen more provided it as a possibility. The only punishment that a captain was not allowed to award on his own judgement was the capital sentence (carried out by hanging from the yard-arm); this required the sanction of a court-martial.

Any officer was empowered to order minor punishments without permission from the captain; one such was 'gagging', the usual deterrent for 'answering back' or contradicting an officer. Tied to a convenient stanchion, the man would have an iron marline spike wedged between his jaws like a horse's bit, fastened by spun yarn knotted at the back of his neck. Soon, lips and gums would be bruised, sore and bleeding but there would be no respite until whoever had ordered the punishment decided that the crime had been expiated. Again, an officer might order a bosun's mate, 'Start that man!' Whereupon the 'starter', a hard knotted cord would be produced, to beat the culprit about the head and shoulders. Thought by many to be worse than an ordinary flogging, this form of chastisement was widely used although completely unauthorised; in 1811 it was officially suppressed.

Minor offences, such as not obeying an order quickly enough, were speedily and summarily dealt with by the Bosun and his Mates, but when considering the disciplinary methods of McCulloch's day it is flogging which most readily springs to mind. Although falling by then into relative disuse, it was still quite common for a man to be 'dusted down', a punishment always seriously regarded, to be awarded by the Captain and by no one else. A full dress naval flogging must have been an awesome spectacle:

'The marines fell in upon the poop with their muskets and arms; the junior officers gathered to windward under the break of the poop with the Captain and lieutenants standing on the weather quarterdeck and the ship's company fell in anyhow on the boats and booms on the lee-side of the ship. On the Captain's order "Rig the gratings," the carpenter and his mates

A Midshipman of the Coast Blockade with the North Foreland lighthouse in background.
(from the Lapthorne Collection)

dragged aft two of the wooden gratings used to cover the hatches, placing one flat on the deck and securing the other against the poop rails. This done, the Captain called forth the offender, telling him that he had transgressed the rules of the Service, knowing the penalty. Next came the order "Strip!" 'upon which the man flung aside his shirt and stretched his arms across the upright grating, there to be lashed tight by the quartermasters. On the report "Seized up, Sir!" 'the Articles of War were produced and the Captain read out the one which had been infringed, removing his hat to show respect for the King's commandments, all present doing likewise. Unfastening the red baize bag, a bosun's mate drew out the red-handled cat; on the command "Do your duty!" 'he advances upon the man spread-eagled before him. Drawing the cat's tail through his fingers, he flings back his arm full sweep and begins to flog with all his strength. A sturdy, well-muscled individual, this petty officer knows full well that any sign of leniency on his part may well result in his demotion, if not in his own chastisement. . .'

Three dozen lashes were common, three hundred not unknown; a normally tough, average seaman would reckon to 'take his dozen and get a red-checked shirt at the gangway' with very little fuss: 'nothing but an "Oh" and a few "O my Gods" and then you could put your shirt back on' but, after another twelve, 'the lacerated back looks inhuman,

36

resembling roast beef burnt nearly black before a scorching fire'. Eventually, Nelson and his like-minded 'band of brothers' came to realise that not only was such punishment unnecessary but that it was often counter-productive:

'My firm conviction is, that the bad man was very little the better and that the good man was much the worse. The good man felt the disgrace and was branded for life, his self-esteem was permanently maimed and he rarely held up his head or did his best again.'

Even Nelson was unable to abolish the practice, but it was certainly employed far more discreetly for the known 'floggers' tended to be overlooked when a new ship was commissioned or they might find themselves in command of a noxious prison hulk, or, again, as was Captain William Bligh (late of HMS *Bounty*), be posted to the Antipodes to administer a convict settlement.

For thieving, 'running the gauntlet' was punishment hardly less severe than flogging. The entire ship's company participated in the procedure by forming up in a double line around the main deck, each man being equipped with a 'nettle' — a triple-stranded tarry rope, a yard long and knotted at one end. Stripped to the waist, the malefactor was placed at the beginning of the line; to his front would be the Master-at-Arms (a petty officer responsible for policing the ship) with drawn sword pointed at his throat, to his rear would be two ship's corporals (assistants to the Master-at-Arms) similarly equipped. With an encouraging lash or two from the Bosun's mate's cat, he would start to walk; if he went at anything other than a steady pace, he would be pricked by steel, either at his throat or in the small of his back. Down the double file he would go, urged on by the 'nettles' wielded by his mates. Often the whole body, including the head, would be practically flayed; treatment was Spartan, a dousing by a bucket or two of sea water. With his wounds healed, the man would return to duty 'having purged his offence without a stain on his character'. It was customary that never again would the matter be alluded to by any of the company.

Thus far, an undeniably gloomy picture but it should not be

imagined that the lower deck of those days saw no happy faces for many a contemporary account bears witness to the contrary. Charles Reece Pemberton for instance, later to become an author and actor, was swept up by a Liverpool press-gang at the age of 17 to serve six years (1817-23) at sea. Loathing the general discomfort and the brutality of his initial training, he soon grew to love the frigate to which he was eventually posted:

'My roving dwelling-place, my beloved and beautiful home the *Alceste*, the happiest home I ever knew.'

William Richardson too, gunner in the *Prompte* (originally a French 6th-rater with 20 guns, captured 28th May, 1793 in the Bay of Biscay and eventually broken up in 1813), remembered his old ship with the greatest fondness:

'Where there was none of your brow-beating allowed, nor that austere authority where two men durst hardly to be seen speaking together. . .the crew was like a family united and would, both officers and men, risk their lives to assist each other. . .'

Given the standard of medical and surgical knowledge in those pre-anaesthetic days, a sick or wounded sailor

A frigate under all sail.   E. W. Cooke, 1828.

might — if he were lucky — die mercifully quickly; on the other hand, he might have eventually found himself in a naval hospital at Portsmouth (Haslar), Deal, Paignton, Plymouth or Yarmouth. Besides these major establishments there were smaller treatment centres and sick bays at Belfast, Dartmouth, Douglas, Dover, Dublin, Exmouth, Fowey, Greenock, Hull, Ilfracombe, Leith, Limerick, Lynn, Milford, North Shields, Penzance, Poole and Swansea. Overseas, treatment of a sort would have been found in Antigua, Barbados, Bermuda, Cape of Good Hope, Gibraltar, Halifax, Jamaica, Madras and Malta. The standard of nursing varied enormously and at times it was frankly boisterous:

'The nurses of the hospital were chiefly of the frail sisterhood . . . being accustomed to the manners and associations of sailors, these ladies are extremely bold and audacious and without concern make use of the most indecent observations and actions in their common conversation. . . I had a great deal to do to repulse the temptations I met with from these Syrens.'

(*Adventures of Greenwich Pensioner,* George Watson 1827.)

General hospital discipline too could be rather lax, as the same writer was to find to his cost when, as he was lying in his bed recovering from a fractured femur, two fellow patients came over for a quiet chat:

'Unfortunately, they got into controversy with each other and, growing warm upon it, got to hard names and then to blows. Unluckily for them, and for me too, they each had but one arm and, having none at liberty to support them in their fall, they tumbled with all their weight upon my hapless thigh which at the time was beginning to unite, and it disparted anew.'

On examining him the next day, Watson's kindly surgeon was much perplexed by his patient's relapse, but true to the traditions of the Silent Service, no one — least of all the patient — saw fit to enlighten him.

But to any sailor of that time, the word 'hospital' would have conjured up a vision of the Royal Naval Hospital at Greenwich. Dedicated to the memory of Queen Mary, wife of William III, it was built by Wren in 1696. It was not a hospital in the modern sense but was a large almshouse sheltering and running a pension scheme primarily for disabled seamen, although a few officers were also catered for. By 1815 there

The Royal Naval Hospital, Greenwich circa 1800.

(Now the RN College)　　(From Ireland's *History of Kent*)

were close upon 3,000 'in-pensioners', supervised by a staff of forty headed by the governor (an admiral), a deputy governor, four captains, eight lieutenants, two chaplains, three administrators, a secretary, a cashier, a clerk of the check, an architect and a clerk of the works. To care for the sick, the medical staff comprised a physician, a surgeon, a dispenser-apothecary, six assistants and four matrons (usually officers' widows); all staff were quartered within the hospital. Although in theory any ex-sailor or marine was entitled to a place or to an out-pension, there was a long waiting list and a suitable recommendation from a senior officer was highly desirable. Those lucky ones who did secure a berth were assured of an old age both comfortable and secure, as Lewis *(A Social History of the Navy* 1793-1815) so graphically puts it:

'They were mostly the picked, brine-pickled survivors of a gruelling existence from which the weaklings had long since faded. In the quiet courts and colonnades of the Royal Hospital no enemy stalked them, no likelihood of fatal accident, no sudden onset of sea-disease, not even a nagging fear for tomorrow's bread: only Old Age.'

These hoary old stalwarts were granted free board and lodging plus one shilling a week pocket money. They lived in 'wards' supervised by pensioner boatswains (paid 2/6 weekly) and pensioner bosun's mates (1/6 weekly). Uniform was provided, a blue tail-coat and breeches, a cocked hat and blue stockings; should a man be deemed 'frail and elderly' he could also count on a great-coat. Nightgowns, bedding and neckerchiefs were also issued. Defaulters were required to don a red-sleeved yellow coat until they had atoned for their misdoings. Many inmates lived to a ripe old age; octogenarians were common and in 1803 there were 16 into their nineties and one centenarian. It was not always necessary to have served a lifetime in the navy to become an in-pensioner. Dennis Manning* for example had served just three years in the Coast Blockade as a young man but when he fell incurably ill in late life he was taken in to spend the last seventeen years of his life there.

* See Appendix A

Ships lost in the Royal Navy 1793-1815, compared with enemy losses

	OURS				THEIRS		
No. of guns	Wrecked/ Foundered	Burnt/ Blew up	Total lost A	B	Total lost A	B	Added to RN
100 plus	—	1	1	—	9	—	
98	2	1	3	—	—	—	
80	—	1	1	—	19	12	83
74	13	4	17	1	87	—	
64	5	1	6	—	24	—	

Above are 'Ships of the Line'

50	5	—	5	1	9	—	
44/40	4	1	5	1	94	—	
38/36	38	—	38	6	80	12	162
32	17	1	18	2	37	—	
28	7	—	7	—	18	—	
Total	91	10	101	11	377	24	245

NB Craft mounting less than 28 guns—sloops, brigs and smaller-are not included.

A—lost in action; B—lost by accident.

Dover Castle.
"Seven days past, a Dover cutter landed goods under the Castle . . ."
(Report to Admiralty 1745.)

The Hierarchy

*Take my advice and never go to sea
And you'll become a Ruler of the Queen's Navee!*
(W. S. Gilbert 1836-1911, *HMS Pinafore*.)

Most Naval Commissioned Officers or Sea Officers (until 1858, a Naval Officer was an Admiralty dockyard official) were firmly rooted in the upper and middle classes, although they were not so tightly aristocratic as the army. Many followed their fathers' calling, others were sons of the clergy, army officers, doctors and civil servants. Few, very few, 'came aft through the hawse-hole (an aperture in the bows of a ship through which the cables passed), as the process of rising from the lower deck (the province of the ranks or ratings) was aptly, if inelegantly, described. Many were younger sons without much hope of an inheritance; their only chance of acquiring a reasonable competence (apart from marrying it) was to capture as many enemy ships in as short a time as possible; by this means wealth, in the shape of a share in the prize money, was bound to accrue.

There were five grades of Sea Officer. First stood the Flag Officers, the Admirals of all grades; next below them were the Captains of Post rank commanding ships of the line. Then came the Commanders, captains of smaller vessels, along with the Lieutenants who held commands smaller still (bomb-ketches, gun-brigs, rocket boats and the like) or else occupying subordinate posts on the big ships. Finally, a class on their own, were the Marine Officers who commanded the 'sea-soldiers' — about a quarter of the larger ship's company — responsible for internal security, landing parties and snipers (sharpshooters) on the upper decks in close action.

In his fledgling days, a young officer was advanced by 'interest', the patronage of a person who mattered in the eyes of the Admiralty, perhaps an uncle who was also an Admiral, or a family friend of standing in the City, the Customs or the Treasury. At this stage, seniority mattered little, it was friends that counted but, having secured his Post Captaincy, the aspiring Admiral would find a very different set of rules; from that moment on he would not be permitted to overtake, nor to be overtaken by, anyone on the promotion ladder; gross misconduct (usually cowardice in the face of the enemy), voluntary retirement or death were the only reasons for removal from the game. These regulations had a grossly clogging effect; Nelson, for instance, a Rear-Admiral at 40, would not have attained the top rank of Admiral of the Fleet until 1844 — at the age of 86! To make matters even worse, Post Captains and above were not affected by the run-down of the fleet in 1812 (see p.13) although this promotional bottle-neck was alleviated to some extent when the Midshipman entry was regulated some years later.

In a ship of the line, the Captain stood at the apex of command with his Lieutenants directly beneath him — on 'first-raters' there would be up to eight or nine, all with their specific responsibilities. Next were the Marine Officers and below them — far below — the embryo Sea Officers, the Midshipmen 'young gentlemen' of very little immediate account but of great potential importance; none save these had much hope of walking the quarterdeck of a ship of His Majesty's Navy.

A long drop then in social standing to the Warrant Officers of wardroom status (the wardroom being the Lieutenants' quarters). All Warrant Officers were appointed by the Admiralty, some rising from the Lower Deck and others, such as the Surgeon and the Chaplain entering suitably qualified from civilian life. The most senior, classed by Professor M. Lewis as 'nearly but not quite Gentlemen' were the Master, responsible for navigating the ship (the Captain directing her in action), the Surgeon, the Purser and the Chaplain. Below them, the junior Warrant Officers not of Wardroom status — perhaps they could be regarded as 'almost nearly but not quite Gentlemen', but, whatever their social standing, there is no denying their importance; Captains, Lieutenants

*Naval General Service Medal
1793-1840.*
Daniel Tremendous McKenzie would
have received this medal (see below). A
true 'son of a gun' would not only have
been born 'beneath the barrel of a 32
pounder' but, more than likely, he would
have been conceived there also.

and Masters would come and go but the triumvirate of Bosun,
Gunner and Carpenter was practically sempiternal for, come
what might, they, the Standing Officers stayed with the ship as
if, like the figurehead, they had been built into her. They were
allowed the considerable privilege of having wives and families
living on board with them—hence the award of the Naval
General Service medal to that true 'son of a gun' Daniel
Tremendous McKenzie born in HMS *Tremendous* during the
action of Ushant (the Glorious First of June 1794) and
similarly to Jane Townsend who fought the guns alongside her
husband in HMS *Defiance* at Trafalgar, although some
authorities state that her claim for the medal was refused by
the Admiralty on the grounds that:

'Many women in the fleet were equally useful.'

Stretching out below the Warrant Officers was that vast
concourse, the rest of the ship's company usually known to
their officers as 'The People', stiffened by that notorious

(From the Lapthorne Collection)

Almost nearly but not quite a Gentleman? (see page 44)

A Boatswain of the Royal Navy circa 1810. Always carried (although not shown in this picture) a rattan cane which was used to great effect: 'This small stick of his has wonderful virtue in it and seems little inferior to the rod of Moses, of miraculous memory; it has cured more of the Scurvy than the Doctor, and made many a poor Cripple take up his Bed and walk; sometimes it makes the Lame to skip and run up the Shrouds like a Monkey'.

(Ward, E. *Wooden World Dissected*)

backbone without which no ship of His Majesty's Navy could have ever sailed, let alone fight — the Petty Officers, the armourers, the sailmakers, and 'those brutal men with too much power' the highly respected Quartermasters. Only in action did the Officers and the People 'weld into a fearsome fighting machine'; at all other times there was very little contact between the two worlds.

The People at Work

Our seaman people are more licentious than those of other nations; the reason is, they have less religion. (Rear Admiral Sir Richard Kempenfelt 1718-82.)

For the daily work routine, the company divided into shifts or watches, ensuring that at all times some worked while others rested. The simplest division was into starboard and larboard (replaced by 'port' in 1844) watches, but other Captains preferred the 'three-watch' system and some tried four. The most senior members of the ship's company were the Gunner's and Bosun's Mates, along with those highly respected elderly denizens of the forecastle, tried and trusted in their duties concerned with the anchors, the bowsprit and the foreyard. The whole crew's morale could be judged by the state of the fo'c'sle which was traditionally 'the cleanest and trimmest place in the whole ship'. After the fo'c'sle men came the 'topmen'—young, smart and acrobatic, their highly perilous and exacting task was to work the three masts above the lower yards. Away below them, metaphorically and literally, were the men of the afterguard who worked the lower yards and served the guns in action; 'usually poor seamen and despised by real sailors', they could in their turn look down their noses at the largest division of the ship's company, the 'waisters' or 'men without art or judgement' who, living in the 'waist' of the ship, performed those highly essential but equally unglamorous and unskilled tasks of 'servicing' the others; sometimes these were ordinary seamen too stupid to be trusted aloft' but more often they were Landsmen (or Landmen), the lowest possible rating. A third-rater on active service carried about 70 fo'c'sle men, 170 top-men, 100 afterguard and 300 waisters; an Able Seaman was paid £1.13.6 monthly, an Ordinary Seaman £1.5.6 and a Landsman £1.2.6 plus a share in any prize money accruing. Sleeping space at 14″ per man was, to put it mildly, somewhat limited with row upon row of hammocks cramming the whole lower deck, packed like sardines from one side to the other, although it should be realised that not every man would be off duty and occupying his sleeping space at one time; hence the popularity of the three-watch system. Each man had two hammocks, one in use and the other clean; they were changed and scrubbed weekly, being hung up to dry between the masts. In the cold home waters, sailors did not usually remove many garments before 'getting their heads down' and some in fact are reputed to have slept 'all standing, like a trooper's horse'. Through the strength of Professor Lewis's pen, let us vicariously experience the comfortless situation:

'It is not pleasant to linger over horrors. Yet we are out to delineate life on the lower deck and must not altogether evade our duty. What then, was the state of the lower deck on, say, the first dirty night when a newly commissioned ship was beating down-Channel into a stiff wind and a heavy sea — rolling, pitching, lurching, shuddering? Not by any means were all the Able Seamen and Ordinary Seamen good sailors and it may be presumed that most Landsmen were bad ones. . . let imagination hover for an instant over that tightly wedged mass of retching men who could not even swing in their hammocks. Or again, let us envisage a very common occurrence on some stations — a widespread outbreak of bowel trouble among seamen whose only "accommodation" was the wind-buffeted, wave-washed bows far overhead. Let us at least think, without attempting to put our thoughts into words, what happened. . . perhaps then we should the more honour the memory of those who stuck it out through the years. . .' *Having once sailed as a totally inept Landsman in the 'Winston Churchill' across the North Sea in winter, the Author heartily concurs with these sentiments.*

For their meals, the crew split again into Messes, each Mess comprised four to six men at a narrow table which hooked up onto overhead beams when not in use. Each man paid for his own crockery which was kept in a mess kid or wooden tub secured to the ship's side. All took a weekly turn helping the Cook in the galley, drawing rations daily per man as follows: biscuit, beef or pork 1lb, beer 1 gallon, peas and oatmeal ¼ pint of each, cheese 1½ozs, sugar and butter 1oz each, rum ½ pint neat but diluted to 'grog' before issued (in 1824, tea could be drawn in lieu of half the rum ration and in the year following, cocoa also was allowed). By all accounts, the food was terrible; Professor C. Lloyd of the Royal Naval College Greenwich, speaking in 1980 at a Symposium, *'Starving Sailors',* thought so:

'The records of the Victualling Board demonstrate that the official scale of provisions in the British Navy was generous. Information as to what was actually consumed is more difficult to obtain, but it is certain that the depredations of pursers, rats and weevils and inadequate storage meant that sailors received far less than their official allowance; there may also have been unofficial supplements to their diet, several authors mention *rats which peppered and grilled taste good.* We may wonder at the awful food provided for sailors at a time when the British Navy was gaining its greatest triumphs, but there is some evidence that it was better than that available either to landsmen or to other navies. . .'

Here one should remember the sailor's staple diet, the notorious ship's biscuits. Cooked in the dockyard bakeries, these were round, thick, well-baked objects weighing about

4ozs each, made from wheat and pea flour sometimes adulterated with bone dust. The centre of the biscuit, harder and more compressed than the remainder, was known as 'the reefer's nut' and was usually pitched over the side. Often the biscuit was pounded to crumbs in a pillowcase then mixed with chopped meat and baked, or it could be mixed with sugar and pork fat to make a delectable cake. On a long passage in a hot climate the biscuit became infested by weevils; rebaking sometimes remedied this:

'but the most common custom was to leave the creatures to their quiet and to eat the biscuit at night when the eye saw not and the tender heart was spared'.

His Mess was the only place wherein a man might fully relax; it was always kept scrupulously clean. Politics, quarrelling and incitement to mutiny were rigorously barred therein and anyone indulging risked expulsion from his Mess. A man not able to get on with his messmates could appeal for a change to the First Lieutenant on the first Sunday of the month. Extra prickly characters might pass from Mess to Mess until, having disgusted all hands, they were obliged to eat alone. Uniform as we know it today was not brought in until 1857 and until then, as with the ship's decor, much depended on the Captain's personal taste and whim:

'Some Captains went to strange lengths to gratify their tastes. . .the gig's crew of *Harlequin* were dressed up as harlequins. . .to the great delight of the rest of the ship's company';

Another gig's crew was fitted out with kilts and bonnets and had thistles embroidered on their jackets. For outside work in foul weather, a short coat and a thick apron of leather, felt or tarred canvas, reaching below the knee, were worn.

Ordinary low shoes and thick woollen stockings were preferred to the long sea-boot; they were much lighter and just as waterproof. In dry conditions the usual working rig was white duck or blue cloth trousers and a yellow jacket; the trousers were sometimes blue and white striped. A fur cap with let-down earflaps was popular, others adopted a battered beaver or a low felt with a curly brim. Another fashion in headgear was a turban, twisted from a red or yellow kerchief, others preferred woollen nightcap but whatever the style it was always worn well back off the brow — 'one cannot run up a rigging with a hat jammed over one's eyes'.

For shore leave, Jack loved to dress up in smart or 'tiddley' rig — a short blue jacket ablaze with brass buttons shining like gold, trousers in blue or white cut extremely loose and a trifle over-long, almost covering feet encased in white silk stockings and black leather pumps adorned with huge silver buckles. A black silk scarf might encircle the waist, or else a leather belt carrying a sheath knife. The shirt allowed great scope for cutting a further dash; some would elect for blue and white stripes, others opting for a white background with large red and blue spots. Still others followed the Byronic style with a black silk kerchief knotted loosely at the throat. Long, low-cut waistcoats were in great vogue in scarlet kerseymere, canary yellow or striped and spotted in every colour imaginable. Both jacket and waistcoat were often further embellished by adding sewn-on ribbons 'giving a more gay effect'.

Topping off the *ensemble* was the shore-going hat, made out of tarpaulin and kept glossily black with the regular application of tar and oil, 'cut in a shape dimly resembling the tophats worn by bishops and busmen, but with a more knowing rake'. From this creation would dangle a ribbon bearing the name of the ship in white lettering; it is interesting to note that in some contemporary illustrations the letters HMS prefixing the name of the ship do not occur. In those days, nobody wore whiskers — 'a hairy man is not to be tolerated' — and all went clean-shaven. Strangely enough, long hair was permitted; it was worn either falling loose upon the shoulders or braided into a queue with grease and black ribbon. The pigtail thus formed is said to have originated with the French and found favour with some because it afforded considerable protection when curled into a pad on top of the head; it reached its height of popularity from 1800 to 1815 and then gradually faded into disuse.

Those who chose not to adopt the pigtail often sported ravishing lovelocks; golden ear-rings too were quite popular, being favoured less for decoration than in the belief that they improved the eyesight. Despite this, some Captains forbade them on the grounds that they were 'un-English'.

A Third-rater

There has been, perhaps, no such beautiful thing upon earth, the work of man's hands, as an old 74 under sail.

(John Masefield 1876-1967.)

The most handy and the most generally used ship of the line was the third-rater; typical of her class was HMS *Ramillies*. After a life of glory, including action with Lord Howe off Ushant (the Glorious First of June 1794) and with Nelson against the Danes at Copenhagen (2nd April 1801) she was to find herself in leaky old age stationed permanently in the Downs off Deal as the floating base of the Coast Blockade.

In her hey-day, carrying a full complement of 640, she could hurl a broadside of over half a ton of cast-iron at any of England's foes within a league or so. Riding high as a house on the water, 170ft long and 50ft broad, she displaced 1,700 tons and, excluding her guns, cost £45,000 to build at Randall's the shipbuilders of Rotherhithe in 1785. A thousand fully grown English oaks were cut for her upper works, and as many again of foreign—cheaper and less durable but acceptable for the purpose—went in below her waterline, suitably sheathed in copper to defeat the gnawing onslaught of the insidious toredo worm. Ships of the Royal Navy were built according to Admiralty Regulations or 'Establishment', ensuring— theoretically at least—that the gear of one would fit another of the same type or rating. The Royal dockyards stocked a range of spare parts—masts, spars, sails, ropes and hawsers—to fit vessels of all classes.

Access to *Ramillies* was gained either by the entry-port on the main deck, with its little brass rail and carved porch, or

HMS Wellington (Captain James Liddell) off Dover 12th August, 1839.
By W. J. Huggins 'Marine Painter to His late Majesty William IV'. *Wellington* was a similar ship to *Ramillies* although built some 30 years later, being launched at Deptford Dockyard in 1816 as *Hero* and almost immediately renamed. In 1862 she was converted into a training ship and again renamed as *Akbar.* She was sold in 1908.
(Reproduced by kind permission of Dover Library)

else by a gangway to the upper deck. On both sides of this gangway was a side-rope, worn smooth by the friction of countless hands. Really important visitors — admirals, civic dignitaries and the like — merited a specially woven rope of white cord or, failing this, the ordinary one would be covered with scarlet or green cloth. Both entrances were guarded by a Marine sentry, resplendent in red coat, white pipeclayed breeches and cross-belts; a Midshipman too would be posted at the gangway to report the approach of all boats to the Lieutenant of the watch.

Once on deck, a visitor would find himself just behind the mainmast, close by a ladder leading up to the quarterdeck, the province of the officer on duty. Above, reached by another ladder, was the poopdeck beneath which were the Captain's quarters, sometimes called the coach-house, often with a skilfully and elaborately carved oaken exterior of gilded cherubs, cornucopiae, drums, banners, wreaths and the Royal Arms. Outside his glazed windows the Captain could walk in private in his quarter-gallery with its gilded rails.

Far at the other end of the ship in the bows was the figure-head, often a carved representation of a mythical personage suggested by the name of the ship, kept immaculate by the crew who would take great pride and pains in reddening lips and cheeks, gilding hair and rendering any further cosmetic service deemed necessary.

The Captain's state apartments where he received and lodged visitors were one of the few places aboard where it was possible to stand upright; under the windows ran a couch with convenient cupboards beneath; opening off the main chamber were two cabins usually quite barely furnished with a fixed table in each flanked by heavy chairs and a swinging cot alongside a wooden wash-stand. The Captain's foul-weather clothes hanging on pegs, a swinging lamp, a telescope on wall brackets, a stand of muskets, a rack of cutlasses and possibly a trophy of arms would provide the only breaks in an otherwise bare expanse of wood panelling. Some exceptional

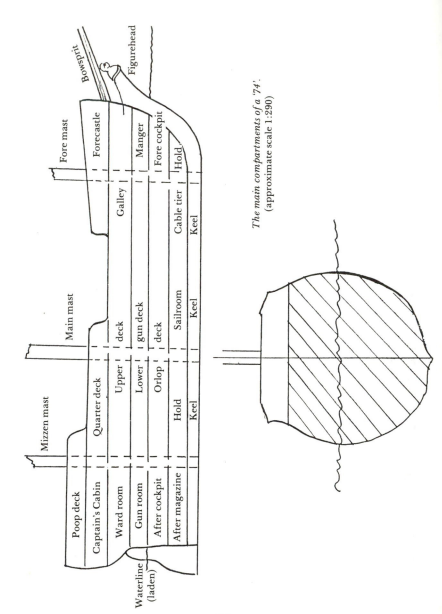

The main compartments of a '74'.
(approximate scale 1:290)

Captains, it is true, contrived to live in great splendour with carpets and Italian oil-paintings; some even burnt incense in silver censers to mask the smell of bilge wafting up from the ship's nether regions, but such men were exceptionally rare and, in general, the Captain who sported anything exceeding a bookcase and a set of curtains was looked at askance, for decorations over and above the absolute minimum were regarded with some suspicion and considered 'Persian and soul-destroying'.

Nelson's favourite external colour scheme persisted much in vogue for many years after Trafalgar; black sides towering above the water-line contrasting strongly with the pale lemon of the gun-port tiers chequered by the port-lids whose outsides were black also. This, the famous 'Nelson chequer', at first permitted only to those who had fought with him in his last battle was eventually allowed to all. Below decks, for grimly obvious reasons, the walls were painted blood-red but after Trafalgar, deviation crept in with green, white, yellow and brown according to the Captain's own preference. The guns, along with many other internal fittings, were painted black, chocolate or red; masts were varnished brown with their blocks, tackle and other rigging appurtenances tarred black. A Frenchman's masts were usually painted black and it was therefore customary before a general engagement (if there was time) for ours to be painted white in an effort to reduce the confusion in battle.

Returning to the interior, the main hatchway led down to the main deck and here, right aft, was where the lieutenants and the senior warrant officers took their meals in the ward-room. Here was space and light, similar to the Captain's apartment but without the stern walk; on each side the quarter galleries were often fitted out as lavatories. Forward from here, the cabins for the senior lieutenants, not much more than elm-panelled cupboards just large enough to contain a cot, a desk and a sea-chest. Nearby were mounted the 24-pounders, half the ship's fire-power and

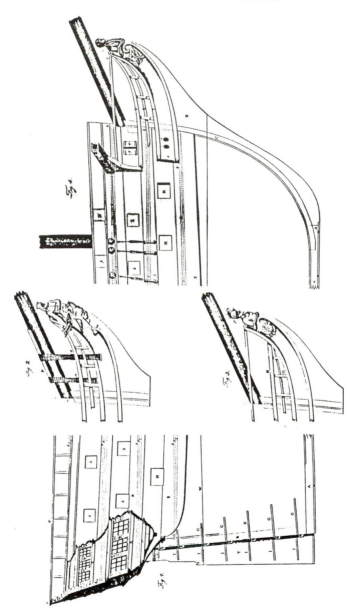

Types of figure-heads, Head and stern of a '74' Gun Ship.
(From Falconer's Marine Dictionary 1769)

midships was the galley, brick-floored as a fire precaution. On the next level down was the lower gun-deck, broadest and stoutest of all—here were the really heavy guns, the massive 34-pounders; here in action the firing was heaviest and hottest and here, naturally, lived the Gunner and his Mates, right aft in the Gun-room which also did duty as the ship's armoury and the most junior Midshipmen's dormitory. On this deck too, the general ship's company slept and ate; right forward was the manger sheltering the livestock carried as a source of fresh meat and also serving as breakwater to prevent the sea pouring along the deck—in heavy weather the animals often drowned.

Down still further was the orlop (overlap) deck, not fully planked over and practically below the waterline. A gloomy place at the best of times, here was the after-cockpit accommodating the senior Midshipmen and the Surgeon's Mates; in action it rapidly transformed into the main operating theatre. Opening off here were the junior lieutenants' the Surgeon's and the Purser's cabins and further forward the kitbag racks and storage space for sails and cables. In the forward cockpit were to be found the Carpenter's and the Bosun's stores, below them the powder hatches; copper-lidded, always padlocked and always under a Marine guard which was doubled when action was imminent. Down in the ship's vast round belly, between the powder magazines, was the main hold containing ballast, provisions and water. Here were to be found also the fish-room, the spirit-room and the bread-room, this last containing an incredible quantity of ship's biscuit—sufficient to last the duration of the cruise.

It was widely believed that our ships were so badly designed, in contrast with the French, that 'they seem to have been built by the mile and a length cut off as required'. This astonishing admission diametrically opposes Masefield's admiration but even he was forced to admit that the most striking feature about a 74 was her elephantine bulk; her true beauty did not become apparent until she had gained momentum in full sail upon her natural element.

The Stern of a '74'.

(From Falconer's Marine Dictionary 1769)

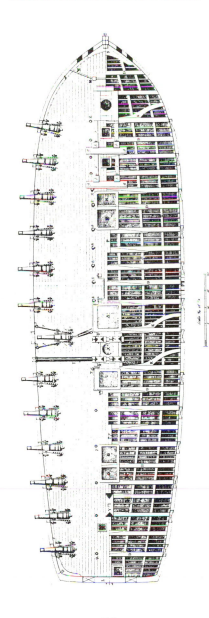

Lower-deck of a '74' Gun Ship.
(From Falconer's Marine Dictionary 1769)

The Coast Blockade

A service whose basis consists in an insidious watchfulness over others and a hostile segregation from their fellow men. (A Naval Sketch Book Capt. W. N. Glascock RN 1832.)

The story of the Coast Blockade for the Prevention of Smuggling falls into three definite phases. First came the experimental days of 1816-18, a period of comparative calm with both sides building up their strength while assessing their opponents' capabilities. Then followed ten years of open confrontation, with the Force becoming more land-orientated, although it never entirely forsook its marine origins. This was the time of the major affrays of unprecedented savagery which shook the coast from Sheerness to Newhaven at the end of which both of the major Kent gangs were scattered to the wind. Some say that this was not due to the undoubted effort of the Blockade and that the root cause of the old Trader's eclipse was economic, that the removal of many import duties had made the risks of smuggling simply not worthwhile. The truth of this is debatable but the fact remains that the last major confrontation in which the Blockade was involved was at Bexhill in 1828; there were further affrays but these were fought with the Coast Guard. The final phase was one of rapid dissolution; by January 1830, 350 men were removed from the Kent patrols and in the year following all vessels were posted away or else towed off to an ignominious end in the breaker's yard. By the spring of

1831, the newly reformed Coast Guard took over completely; Flogging Joey and his Warriors faded rapidly into Kent coast folklore.

Early Days

After so long a period of war in every part of Europe, many of the most daring professional men discharged from their occupation and adverse to the daily labour of agriculture or mechanical employment will be the ready instruments of those desperate persons who have a little capital and are hardy enough to engage in the trade of smuggling.

This extract from a Treasury paper of 1815 forecasts the position with great accuracy, but plans had already been laid to counter the predicted upswing:

'In November 1814, Captain Thos Renwick RN became impressed with a conviction that measures more efficacious might be rendered practicable for the suppression of smuggling. He accordingly in March 1815 developed his ideas on the subject to the Board of Admiralty and proposed a plan which secured so much attention that it became the foundation of the present system of the Coast Guard. . .' *O'Byrne's Naval Biographical Dictionary* (1849).

Allowing Renwick to be the Coast Blockade's progenitor, the title of midwife must surely be given to Captain William McCulloch RN (1782-1825) whose sobriquet gives this book its title. Third son of the laird of Barholm, a village on the Kirkcudbrightshire coast, he did not join the Navy until the advanced age of 16. He learned his profession in the usual hard way, much of his early service being with the Channel Fleet blockading the French ports 'in those storm-beaten ships on which the Grande Armée never looked'. These were the ships which stayed at sea for years at a stretch, coming into port only when nothing more could be devised by the ingenuity of their own crews to keep them serviceable. Here, then, he gained the invaluable experience upon which he was to draw in later years in his campaign against the smugglers. His immediate destiny, however, lay across the Atlantic with the outbreak of war in 1812 with the United States finding him in command of the sloop *Heron* on the Leeward Islands

61

St Leonard's Church, Upper Deal.
Capt. McCulloch was buried here 29th October, 1825.
(Reproduced by kind permission of Ivan Green)

The Port Admiral's Residence Queen St., Deal (demolished 1936).
(Photograph taken circa. 1920, reproduced by kind permission of S. W. Hulke Esq.)

station. During the following two years in this area he captured one Yankee privateer and several merchantmen. Awarded his post-Captaincy in 1814, he was very shortly after given command of the Admiral's flagship, the brand-new frigate *Barossa*. Returning to England in 1815, he was appointed to another frigate *Ganymede* taking station in that notorious stretch of the Channel, the Downs off Deal, so much abhorred by Nelson ('such weather I never saw in my life. . . nothing but wrecks all over the coast'). Now it was that he began his campaign against the smugglers of Kent and Sussex — a struggle which death alone forced him to conclude.

63

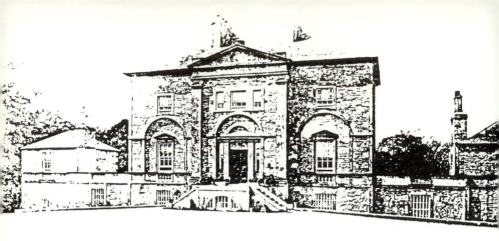

Barholm House, Kirkcudbrightshire.
Captain McCulloch's birthplace, the house was built in 1747 to accommodate the family when it moved down from its castle, some five miles distant. (see page 146)

It is a curious paradox that although Capt. McCulloch became the scourge of the Channel smugglers, both his father and grandfather had no doubt, like all the Galloway lairds, made a very good thing out of smuggling on the Solway which was particularly well adapted for the purpose, being very near the Isle of Man where bulk cargoes could be broken up and the goods transferred to smaller, faster, craft. In 1786, the Commissionaire of Customs wrote to the Sherif of Kirkcudbrightshire mentioning:

'Your smuggling gentlemen who have smuggling harbours on their estates and who do, I suppose, taste the sweets of this illicit trade and do everything in their power to encourage it and are actually stopping up all access to these favoured spots but to those who carry on the illegal importations . . .'

The log of HMS *Ramillies* mentions his passing but briefly:

'25th October 1825, Capt. McCulloch departed this life.'
'29th October 1825, Capt. McCulloch interred 12.30 hrs, Lieuts Searle and Williams attending.'

This conciseness is, perhaps, only to be expected of an official naval record; what is more remarkable is the scant attention paid by the local press:

'Oct 25th, at the Port Admiral's residence*, Deal, after a long and afflicting illness, Wm McCulloch Esq, Captain of His Majesty's Ship *Ramillies* and commanding the 1st, 2d and 3d divisions of the coast blockade'(sic).

*See note page 65

A simple wall tablet in the burial ground of St. Leonard's Church, Upper Deal, enlightens one very little more:

'Sacred to the memory of Captain William McCulloch RN of Barholm, Scotland, who departed this life on the 25th October 1825. Age 45 years.'

It is noteworthy that all reference to his past undoubted service to King and Country are omitted; his last command is not mentioned neither is his wife Jane (whom he had married in Antigua in 1810) nor their eight children, all of whom had been christened either in Deal or Walmer. When a serving Captain died, his officers and men would sometimes contribute towards a memorial—no sign of such a practice here. Why such reticence bordering upon anonymity? Was the entire Blockade Force so unpopular or was it that McCulloch was so personally disliked (it should be remembered that he had once promised to make grass grow in the streets of Deal) that no-one was particularly perturbed at his departure? *The Times* certainly ignored his demise.

* This was a gracious building (*ca* 1740) also known as Admiralty House. It stood in Queen Street until it was demolished in 1936, the Classic Cinema being built on the site.

It had large windows, heavy doors and a pillared and porticoed entrance.

A magnificent mahogany staircase led up to the billiards room on the first floor; the pine-panelled dining room could seat 30 with ease. There was also a strong-room with a domed ceiling and a marble floor. Here was stored the fleet's pay plus the bullion often landed at Deal—in 1813 for instance, HMS *Bedford* deposited twenty-five tons of gold and silver in bars, dust and coin. In that same year $2,000,000 worth of Jamaican gold was taken in.

Jerrold, writing in 1907 *(Highways and Byways in Kent)* tells how:

'A little more than a hundred years ago there was said to have been a room here, within a few feet of anything where smuggled goods were housed . . . and where, on one occasion, the wife of the chief official kept a wounded smuggler in until he was nursed back to health and able to make his escape.'

It is difficult to imagine Capt. McCulloch permitting such behaviour to pass unnoticed! By the 1840's, the Admiralty had quit the building; an extra storey was added and a school established. After some time, a well known local doctor made it his home and it was occupied by his family until it was demolished.

A Hard Man?

Was 'Flogging Joey' truly the monster he has so often been depicted? Did he really act 'like a Mediterranean slave-master, driving his men to their duty with the cat at their backs' as one contemporary report has it, or would it be fairer to describe him, as a later authority does, as 'suitably taut'? Was his grim reputation put about by the local free-traders — and were they supported in this by the newly active social reformers? One can hardly credit that he would have had time to organise many full-scale punishment parades as previously described, but did he allow more latitude than was reasonable to his senior petty officers — were, for instance, the Quartermasters unofficially equipped with 'starters'? The truth now will never be known but at the time questions were asked in Parliament and the matter ventilated at all levels, both local and national:

'Sir, I can not resist the impulse in communicating to you, for the benefit of the poor suffering men, deeds fit for the barbarous countries of Africa only in their savage state. The Coast Blockade on the Kent and Sussex coast has been made the subject of the observations and animadversions of several Members of Parliament. . .but success has not attended their efforts because it has been very evident that the system has in great measure checked smuggling on this part of the coast, although at an enormous expence. The men who compose the great body are driven to their duty with the cat at their backs, and for the least deviation from duty are thrown into the hold, ironed, and kept there until the pleasure of their Commander be known. Would you believe it? There were no less than twenty-six of these poor creatures tied up and flogged yesterday, their cries were piercing and reached Rye. Can people do otherwise than feel for them? They are human beings, but if brutally used, they themselves become brutal and hence it is that they attack passengers in the way described by Hon. Members. . .'

The officers of the Coast Blockade reacted strongly to criticism, both verbally and in print, with their customary vigour; nevertheless it has to be recognised that these strictures carried weight in many quarters and even Lord Teignmouth second to none in his staunch defence of the Force — had to admit that 'terrorism in the guise of discipline had crept in during the French wars and had crystallized into recognised custom under certain officers.'

66

But was Captain McCulloch one of these? A search of statistics does little to clarify the situation, for the first readily available returns of corporal punishment in the Royal Navy were not published until 1834, ten years too late to assist in solving this particular problem. Resort to the ships' logs—many are still preserved—wherein were recorded all Captain's punishments could be made, comparing 'Flogging Joey's' score with a random sample taken from other logs. At the end of this dauntingly tedious task one would be little nearer the truth, for only the formal official floggings would be accounted for and the presumably far more common 'startings' and the activities of the Bosun ('the man with the ratten cane') would never have been committed to written record. How, then, to provide as true a portrait as possible of the man? His reports to the Admiralty and other correspondence may still be read and it is from these letters that a vivid picture springs to life from the now faded copperplate hand of his writer or naval clerk.

Captain William McCulloch appears as a man dedicated to the Royal Navy as an institution, if not to the individual sailor under his command. Some of his letters display a sardonic sense of humour while others convey the impression that he was possessed of an extremely practical turn of mind; no doubt today he would have been a keen DIY man. As was the fashion, most of his reports are long-winded affairs, but never, even at his most prolix, was he guilty of mealy-mouthed platitudes. Besides his eternal struggle with the smugglers, his concern with the day-to-day running of his ship is evident; time and again he bombards his masters at the Admiralty with statements, questions and opinions concerning the efficient working, deployment and—significantly—the expansion of his Force; he was a naval workaholic to the day he died. It does seem however that he was little concerned with the personal comfort and well-being of his men; knowing McCulloch's fire-eating propensities, one must applaud the considerable moral courage displayed in the following letter:

67

His Majesty's Ship Ganymede
At Sea 24th December 1815.

Sir,

I beg leave to state to you that a number of Men now in the Sick List are much in need of a proper change of warm cloathing *(sic)* which is essentially necessary to the recovery of their Health. The greater part of the Ship's company under your Command are without a Single change of cloaths, the want of which in this climate at this Season of the year, must contribute to produce a variety of complaints particularly Rheumatism and Catarrh.

I am Sir, Your Obedient humble Servant, *Signed* Chas Miller *Surgeon.*

It is now difficult, if not impossible, to form a final objective judgement of the man's character and behaviour but in making any assessment, the exigencies of the situation and, indeed, the general standards of the day in dealing with the 'lower classes' should be born in mind. It does appear that Kentish smuggling folklore tarred 'Flogging Joey' with a very black brush — even during his lifetime — but, excepting one letter in which he expresses fears for the safety of his young wife and family* there is not the slightest suggestion that this worried him and it certainly never deflected him from his avowed intent to exterminate 'the Illicit Trade', a goal which in the event eluded him as it has every other authority before or since.

Whatever our modern day and age may think of Captain McCulloch, it can never be denied that he pursued his aim to the bitter end. A few weeks before his death he was still hard at work badgering his masters at the Admiralty. On 2nd August 1825, he wrote requesting payment of a long overdue account to a Deal carpenter for the repairs to a Manby's Rocket Firing Apparatus (used to shoot a line from the beach to a ship in distress); that same day he suggests the establishment of a Blockade watch-house at Warden Point, Sheppey. His last recorded act was to nominate a lad as Volunteer 1st Class for entry in his own ship *Ramillies.*

*'About ten days ago, they fired at me on the Walmer Road, of which, as well as many of their acts of abuse and violence, I took no notice. I am convinced that giving way to these ruffians will only encourage them and I am determined not to do it, but I am much distressed at the state of alarm into which my family has been thrown.'

68

McCulloch Makes his Mark

Unless prompt measures are taken immediately for making an awful example of those who have trampled upon every kind of legal authority, the smugglers on all parts of the coast will not hesitate on proceeding to the destruction of those employed in support of the Revenue. (Capt W. McCulloch, Admiralty report 10th February 1817)

McCulloch's first opportunity to hit the smugglers had already been snatched from him in the previous late autumn when a spell of fair weather in the Channel suddenly broke up. Knowing that the smugglers were waiting for just such conditions so that they could make a dash from 'over the other side' (as Dovorians still refer to France), he laid plans to ambush them on the Deal beach. Unfortunately for him, the weather worsened further still into a gale and, being unable to launch his galleys, he was obliged to abandon his plan. The smugglers, however, undismayed by the perils of the ocean and fortified by their far superior local knowledge cheerfully won their first round with the Blockade by proceeding to unload a very profitable 2,500 ankers* of high-class brandy.

Despite this initial setback, the Admiralty was very impressed with McCulloch's attitude and permitted him to develop his theme. Initially, shore parties from his ship the frigate HMS *Ganymede,* stationed in the Downs off Deal, were rowed out at dusk to patrol the cliff tops and beaches between the North and the South Forelands, being withdrawn at daybreak for much needed rest and refreshment. In the very early days of the Blockade, McCulloch had other responsibilities. In 1816 for example it was reported:

'Two Tunisian pirates captured a Hamburg vessel in the North Sea and were chased in vain by *Ganymede* 26, Capt. W. McCulloch.'

With the withdrawal of the two Customs cutters which had previously been patrolling the area, the Royal Naval Coast Blockade for the Prevention of Smuggling was born, although

* The anker was a wooden cask holding 7.5 gallons, the half-anker being smaller was more easily handled and was preferred when men, rather than horses or waggons, were to be used to transport the load over any distance; one man could carry two, one under each arm and further supported by a sling of rope across the shoulders.

'Patrols were moved out at dusk to patrol the cliff tops and beaches . . .' (see page 69)
(Old print 'No-man's Land, Margate')

official recognition was delayed until a Treasury Minute dated 17th June 1817 established its existence.

By April 1817, McCulloch had made his presence felt and was able to report that, despite certain teething troubles, his scheme was already bearing fruit; he particularly commends two junior officers, Newman and Peat (see p.94) whose parties had even now located five 'places of concealment':

"This discovery will, I am assured, be a most severe blow to the smugglers, as they were enabled to remove their cargoes from them in a few minutes and hitherto no person besides themselves could form any idea of the manner in which their store-holes were built. They are generally 4ft. deep, of a square form and built of 2 inch plank, with a scuttle in the top into which a trough filled with shingle is fitted instead of a cover, to prevent their being found out by pricking* and I understand that they were built above two years ago. I have ordered them to be destroyed, and parties are employed for searching for such concealments along the other parts of the beach.'

*A method of searching for buried or otherwise concealed contraband using a lance-like iron rod or 'pricker'.

With *Ganymede* ordered away to Cork, McCulloch transferred to another frigate, the *Severn* (she in her turn to be replaced some years later by *Ramillies* the redoubtable third-rater). Eventually the Preventive Waterguard withdrew entirely from that part of the coast leaving the Coast Blockade in complete control of the shore from Sheppey to Selsey Bill; complete control, that is to say, apart from the Trade which was to become increasingly troublesome. This, however, is anticipating; in the earlier days action was confined to such minor encounters as Laker describes:

In the Downs.

In the days of sail, the Downs—a stretch of shallow and (usually) calm water between the Deal shore and the Goodwin Sands—was a major anchorage, bestowing upon Deal the distinction of being the main harbour town of south-east England. With the coming of steam the significance of the Downs diminished and Deal, with no facilities to offer the steamships, lost its erstwhile importance.

Old Naval Hospital, Deal.
(Reproduced by kind permission of Ivan Green)

'During the closing days of 1817, Captain McCulloch received information that some men intended to remove smuggled goods from a house in Middle Street to another part of the town. He accordingly detailed two young midshipmen from *Severn* to watch the locality. Between 6 and 7 in the evening, the young officers perceived a party of men carrying goods coming along Middle Street, they courageously attacked them and arrested the first man. The second, a boatman named Worthington, threw down his burden and made a bolt for it. The officers gave chase and overtook him in Lower Street near the fish-market; as he offered a desperate resistance they drew their pistols and threatened to shoot. One pistol was discharged (by accident the officer said) and a hostile crowd soon collected. The second midshipman fired his weapon and a young man in the crowd was slightly wounded. The two men then drew their swords to defend themselves but, being no match for the infuriated men attacking them, made a dash for it and took refuge in a neighbouring shop. The Mayor, Edward Iggulsden, hearing the hubbub, was soon on the spot and ordered the officers to be arrested. McCulloch attended the magisterial hearing and gave evidence that the officers were acting in the discharge of their duty and that the whole affair was caused by the resistance offered by the smugglers. The Mayor however, accepting the evidence of his fellow townsmen, committed the midshipmen for trial on a capital charge, refusing bail. . .a few weeks later, the Law Office of the Crown applied for bail which was admitted; three months later the Admiral promoted the young men to lieutenants for good conduct and devotion to duty.'

Soon, McCulloch was able to report to the Admiralty: 'The guard-houses are ready for the reception of the officers and men to be employed on the shore.' This was bad news for the smugglers although regrettably it came too late to raise the morale of two unfortunate crew members of the *Severn* who fell (or were they pushed?) one dark and stormy winter's night over the Broadstairs cliffs. Nevertheless, with the guard-houses spaced out at roughly four-mile intervals, much of the south-east coast now came under Blockade surveillance. Retaining his ships as marine depots, McCulloch took over two large buildings as his main land HQs; one was the old Naval hospital at Deal (now the Royal Marines School of Music) and the other Fort Moncrieff at Hythe, part of the anti-invasion defences erected earlier in the century, now demolished.

The Martello towers, part of the same system but never tried in the crucible of war, were given new life. Four were taken over as signal stations along with thirteen more stations newly built (see endpapers) to link Deal with Beachy Head thus

A Martello Tower at Hythe after artillery practice (1891).
Details of its massive construction are still clearly visible.
(Folkestone Library collection)

permitting rapid (visual) transmission of intelligence and orders along the coast and enabling far closer contact between naval and customs craft operating out to sea. Each signal station was manned by a highly reliable, albeit elderly or disabled, naval lieutenant on half-pay plus 3/- a day, assisted by an equally reliable ancient seaman. The rest of the Martello towers at last justified the cost of their building by accommodating the Blockade land patrols, each taking an officer and ten ratings.

Cobbett (1762-1835) passed by at that time; although he must have seen the 'Warriors' he makes no mention of them but, fiery old radical that he was, he derides their shelters:

'Here has been the squandering, here has been the paupermaking. . . I think I counted upwards of thirty of these ridiculous things, which I daresay cost five, perhaps ten, thousand pounds each. . . I daresay they cost millions' (*Rural Rides* 1823).

In cold fact, the original estimate per tower was £2,000 but then, as now, strikes and inflation played their part to bring the final figure to half as much again. Each tower called for 500,000 bricks which were made at various sites in London, Kent and Essex and brought round by barge to be dumped on the nearest beach — several contractors made reputed fortunes from this work. They were undeniably impressive in their strength and the thickness of the walls (13′ maximum), they were bonded and covered with a substance produced after many rigorous tests by the best brains of the Army — the Royal Engineers at Woolwich. The result was a mixture of lime, ash and hot tallow so resilient that a cannon-ball fired at close range merely bounced harmlessly off and to this day the Martello tower sets problems for restoration experts and demolition workers alike.

The Coast Blockade seamen were usually Landsmen and they often lacked the true sea-going experience; many were Irish labourers 'unskilled though hardy' signing on for a limited period of three years with the Force, to which they were posted after a short course of seamanship under the Bosun of a training ship.

Broadstairs Cliffs. (Old print)
Did they fall — or were they pushed? (see page 73)

76

One such man was Dennis O'Mainnin*. It appears that the true career seaman shunned the Blockade like the plague (despite certain pension allowances) but the petty officers had certainly seen their share of the deep blue sea if Richard Gardiner* is to be taken as typical. So too with the officers; most were experienced and many would have been kicking their heels on half-pay had it not been for the Kent and Sussex smugglers. Whatever their personal views on their Captain's disciplinary methods, it is certain that with very few exceptions they were highly practical, courageous men ready to tackle the smuggler wherever and whenever they met up with him. In this, again almost invariably, one finds that they were backed up by their men, although this does not signify that within the Blockade service all was truth, beauty and light! Far from it; apart from considerable recruiting difficulties (the Press Gang having gone out of business long since), bribe-taking and collusion with the smugglers all had to be contended with. The life of a 'Warrior' was uncomfortable, dangerous and lacked glamour; small wonder that some deserted to the Traders.

* See Appendix A

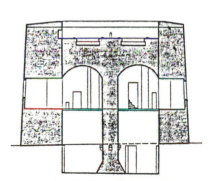

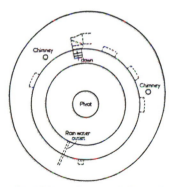

*Section through the tower
No. 23 at Dymchurch, Kent.*

*Plan of the roof or gun platform of
tower No. 23 at Dymchurch.*

(Reproduced by kind permission of J. Floydd Esq. FRIBA)

The Timeball Tower, Deal.
(Old drawing. Reproduced by kind permission of Ivan Green)

The Struggle for Supremacy

Sir W. J. Hope, one of the Lords of Admiralty, accompanied by Sir John Gore, the Port Admiral of Sheerness, is on a survey of the coasts of Kent and Sussex in order to ascertain the expediency of relinquishing or continuing the establishment for the suppression of smuggling entitled the coast blockade.

(The Gentleman's Magazine, June 1821).

It seems that Captain McCulloch not only had to fight the Wicked Trade, he also had the Treasury to contend with. Certain doubts were voiced as to the loyalty, integrity and efficiency of the Blockade, but the authorities were forced to the conclusion that, despite these misgivings, the Service had perforce to be retained:

'The removal at the present time when the smuggler is exerting himself in a peculiar manner to defeat its vigilance, the dangers of any alteration under such circumstances are sufficiently obvious. . .'

Signs of escalating violence soon became manifest. In the Folkestone district the Blockade sentinels were fired upon on four separate occasions (Autumn 1819); soon after there followed a serious affray in which Lieut Dickenson acquitted himself so gallantly as to elicit the approbation of the Commander in Chief the Nore and the Board of Admiralty. At Stangate Creek on Sheppey, Midshipman Francis Baker was attacked by 300 smugglers and left for dead; these were the opening scenes of the bloody battle of attrition looming ahead to stretch menacingly over the next decade and more.

The Coast Guard was established in 1821 and a compliment of sorts was paid to the Coast Blockade, the coasts of Kent and Sussex being specifically excluded from the remit of the new organisation and left entirely to McCulloch's force which, naturally, took its orders not from Customs House but direct from the Admiralty. Henceforward, attack was to be the watchword:

'We think, indeed, that from the moment when a disposition has been made by the smugglers to offer an organised and armed resistance to the military and civil functions of the public, the force directed against them should be such as to leave them neither chances nor hopes of success . . .' (Treasury Report)

Sandgate Castle (near Folkestone, Kent).
Originally part of Henry VIII's coastal defence system, this building was renovated to become part of the Coast Blockade network.
(Folkestone Library collection)

Sandgate from the Sea.

Note the cliff-top line of Martello towers and the semaphore signalling station (see page 73) below which, on the shoreline, Sandgate Castle is clearly visible.

(Folkestone Library collection)

An Account of the Expense incurred in other Departments for the service of the Coast Blockade in each Year from the first Institution of the Preventive Water Guard to the close of 1829: prepared pursuant to the directions of the Right Honorable the Lord Viscount Melville, of the Right Honorable the Lords Commissioners of the Admiralty as required on a Parliamentary return of the 16 August 1828, (see Treasury's letter of the 12 April 1830)

	1818	1819	1820	1821	1822	1823	1824	1825	1826	1827	1828	1829	Total
	£	£	£	£	£	£	£	£	£	£	£	£	£
England	29,513	34,752	42,934	57,258	144,613	146,326	82,127	106,755	87,418	82,936	83,122	83,065	777,224

Navy Office
11 May 1830

The Blockade's Budget.
Note the staggering increase in 1825 — the year following the extension of the Blockade.

TABLE: The Comparative Strengths and Costs of the Customs Departments 1820

Department	Strength	Salaries
The Landguard of Riding Officers	157	£ 19,507.17. 1
The Preventive Waterguard	1,250	£ 92,003. 9. 2
HM Ships	2,375	£154,399. 0. 0
Revenue Cruisers		
Admiralty controlled	1,553	£158,089. 8. 1
Customs controlled	97	£ 7,373. 3. 3
HM Coast Blockade	1,276	£ 89,152. 8. 4
Totals	6,708	£520,525. 5.11

Expansion leads to Escalation

Be pleased to acquaint the Lord Commissioners of the Admiralty. . . that I should be fully prepared to occupy the new line of Coast in one month from receipt of their Lordships' Order to that effect. (Letter from Capt McCulloch to the Admiralty headed HMS *Ramillies*, Downs, 7th March 1824.)

The 'new line' referred to was the extension north to take in the Isle of Sheppey and south along the Sussex coast, both areas up until then had been under Coast Guard control; much to Captain McCulloch's annoyance:

'I am entirely prevented from carrying into effect the arrangements I had made for blockading that Island which in fact at present is not guarded at all.'

Now the pressure was on and the smugglers,

'Finding it impracticable to elude the vigilance of their opponents and driven to distress by the suppression of the contraband trade, had no other choice than a desperate resort to the use of armed associations; several powerful gangs were organised accordingly.

Firearms had in fact already been employed for some years, their first recorded use having been by the North Kent gang at Reculver in the summer of 1820 in a clash with a

Turner's painting (1825) depicts Deal as Captain McCulloch would have known it. To the left, hovelling luggers are being run out to the wreck on the extreme right. The signal flags were owned by shipping companies to communicate with their vessels anchored in the Downs. Left centre is the Royal Hotel — then known as the Three Kings — where Nelson stayed while conducting one of his lesser known (and less successful) operations against the French in 1801.

Blockade patrol led by Lieut Douglas; a midshipman and several seamen were wounded, but there were no arrests and the smugglers withdrew carrying their casualties. Five months later, the South Kents followed suit; at Sandgate near midnight on the 8th November a galley carrying spirits, tobacco and salt, said to be from Boulogne, crunched onto the shingle whereupon it was straightaway surrounded by two hundred smugglers. Fanning out into the usual formation for the unloading of goods, they were challenged by two Blockade sentinels. Reacting violently, they shot James Walker in the groin and bludgeoned David Sheahan. Hearing the firing, Lieut Peat sprang out of hiding and dashed into the fray accompanied by his orderly, John Green. After a stiff fight, Green was captured but Peat, despite a leg wound, hacked his way clear by cutlass, although he was not able to prevent the smugglers carrying off the goods. Within two days, a Crown agent slipped into Hythe to collect evidence but after a month had to admit failure:

'As most of the inhabitants of Folkestone, Hythe and Sandgate are connected with the smugglers, many of them supposed to have been assisting on this occasion, no information can be obtained or expected from them. . .'

He was perfectly correct; neither discoveries nor arrests were ever made.

Baiting the Blockade

Innumerable instances of opposition to the exertion of Excise Officers on the part of the Folkestone magistrates may be proved. . . Addendum to the Folkestone Excise Officer's Report by Lieut P. Graham RN of the Coast Blockade 27th December 1823.

It was painfully apparent that the Folkestone Bench held the Blockade in some contempt and that this attitude was heartily reciprocated. Every artifice to thwart the Preventive men was adopted; the case of Thomas Godden is typical. His house was searched on 27th March 1822; one half-anker of white brandy, two empty half-ankers and a pint bottle of colouring matter being discovered therein, the significance being that brandy was always imported 'white' i.e. colourless, colouring (burnt sugar solution) being added by the Customs after the duty had been paid. It therefore follows that any 'white' brandy discovered must have been illegally imported. The case was duly brought before the Folkestone magistrates and it having been proved, one Mr James Major, surgeon-apothecary of that town (he later became Mayor) produced a certificate stating that the brandy was 'an absolute necessity for the cure of scrofulous condition with which the Family of the aforesaid Thomas Godden was afflicted' and that he himself had prescribed the cure. Questioned as to whether white brandy was absolutely necessary, he replied that it was.

In consequence, the fine was reduced from £100 to £2, and the seizing officer's reward from £10 to 4/- (20 pence). On another occasion, the same officer called upon Mr Henry Butcher, another Folkestone magistrate, to procure a warrant to search a house for contraband. Mr Butcher immediately adopted delaying tactics, despatching his servant girl to warn the suspect:

'Mr Butcher left his parlour under the pretence of looking for a Testament to administer the accustomed Oath, although he, the said Magistrate, at the time he was speaking, was resting his hand on a Bureau on which lay a Testament which he, the said Magistrate, could not avoid *seeing distinctly* as he was first looking there for it. . .'

Later that year, 1½ gallons of colouring matter were seized at the sign of the North Foreland in Folkestone, kept by James Mace:

'To this House the Magistrates of the Town daily resort to drink and smoke pipes, in consequence of which they. . . were much biased in Mace's favour so that when he was brought before them, and the offence being proved, they mitigated the Penalty of *Two Hundred Pounds* to so low as *one fourth,* and they, the Magistrates, subsequently petitioned the Commissioners of Excise in favour of the Offender, and the said Commissioners were pleased to place so much reliance on the honour of the Magistrates as to leave a further mitigation to their discretion, and they in consequence fined the said James Mace in the sum of *Twenty Shillings* only!

By these means the Excise Officer was to see his computed

86

award drop first from £20 to £5 and finally to 2/- (10 pence)!

The unkindest cut of all was still to come. A few weeks later:

'I ascertained that a Woman named Smith was about to commence keeping a Public house in Folkestone. Knowing she was the Widow of a man who commanded a large smuggling Lugger which was lost last Winter, I considered it my duty civilly to express a hope that she would be particular in her observance of the Excise Laws.'

Word of this was soon to reach the hypersensitive ear of the Folkestone Bench and the unfortunate officer was called to give account for his over-zealousness:

'I was called to the Town Hall, where Mr Hobday, who was on the Bench, abused me in a very violent manner for having spoken to the Woman aforesaid and proceeded to such lengths that another Magistrate named Hart was obliged to interfere to stop him.'

It was, however, the affair of William Poskett which really brought matters to a head, resulting in an inquiry ordered by the Home Secretary, Sir Robert Peel, himself. He had received a complaint from the Folkestone magistrates regarding the conduct of 'One, P. Graham, Lieutenant of HM Navy and serving in the Coast Blockade'. It seems that on 12th September 1823, Poskett was charged at Folkestone with:

'Making a light by a contrivance or device called a Lanthorn on or from part of the Coast or Shores of Great Britain or within Six miles of such Coast or Shore for the purpose of making or giving a Signal to some Person or Persons on board a Smuggling Ship Vessel or Boat.'

The prosecution, in accordance with regulations, was conducted by Lt Graham who called, as his chief witness, a Blockade Seaman, Richard Jones who stated that while patrolling the beach in East Wear Bay during the hours of darkness, he heard a noise on the shingle. He walked across to investigate, saw a light shine out and a man running away. He chased and caught the man whom he identified as the prisoner. He picked up a lantern some two feet away from the prisoner, but could find nothing on him by which a light might have been struck. Poskett resisted arrest, offering to fight witness and declaring that he was a gamekeeper out after rabbits. Questioned by the prosecution, witness asserted that he saw the defendant shine a light out to sea. The Bench enquired whether the prosecution had any further evidence to support this assertion but, there being none, the case was dismissed Lt Graham in a written report to Captain McCulloch states:

'Poskett is a man of most notorious Smuggling habits belonging to Folkestone. Having taken him before the Bench for showing a light contrary to the Act 47 George III Chapt 66 Sec 34, I am accused of having interrupted and corrected Richard Jones in his examination and it is said that I told the Magistrates "I know the Law as Well as you do" and behaved so as to provoke the Bench to tell me that I never should appear before them again in the character of Prosecutor — all of which I deny most positively.'

Mr Graham consumes a further six large sheets of Admiralty writing paper in his defence, describing the Magistrates' Clerk, with whom he had previously clashed as:

'A very perplexed, ill-tempered man who rose, and with the most provoking gestures as well as language, accused me of putting words into the witness's mouth.'

After Poskett's release, Graham continues;

'This same man remarked, in a very violent manner, that the Officers of the Coast Blockade ought to be excluded from the Court during all such examinations as they certainly influenced the Seamen in giving their Evidence by keeping them in dread of punishment. . . I then appealed to the Mayor who replied that this was his opinion also and telling me then, for the first time, that I had asked improper questions. Whereon I left the Court immediately.'

Some days later, Graham met the Mayor out riding. He was about to pass him unacknowledged when:

'He accosted me, nodding his head with a most sarcastic Smile. I expressed a desire to have no communication with him, except on duty, and had passed him when he rode close to me, calling out in a very imperious tone that I was an impertinent fellow and that he should complain to my superiors, laying great stress on the latter word. . . that he would not submit to the impertinence of a Subaltern in the Navy and that I should hear of it again in a manner I should not like, adding that as long as he should remain Chief Magistrate on the Folkestone Bench I should never be admitted into Court as a Prosecutor. . . to this I rejoined that the Subaltern in the Navy (which he had been pleased to call me) was then talking to him as the Folkestone Apothecary and not as the Folkestone Mayor. . .'

And so on. . . and on. . . and on. One is forced to the conclusion that in choosing to join the Royal Navy, Mr Graham deprived the Bar, or possibly the Stage, of a most promising practitioner.

A supporting statement by Lt Samuel Hellard (of whom much more later), Assistant Surgeon Ephraim Gruebke, Admiralty Mate Thomas Brent and Midshipman William Mitchell, all of the Coast Blockade, confirms Graham's statement and emphasises the clerk's unorthodox behaviour in that he:

'Omitted to put down such parts of the Witness's Evidence as would shew that the Prisoner was the person who did shew the light.'

Furthermore, they point out that throughout the whole proceedings

'Lieut Graham conducted himself towards all the Magistrates with the utmost respect and decorum notwithstanding that he was frequently and most unprovokedly addressed most uncourteously by the said Magistrates.'

A parting broadside sweeps Bench, Clerk and the accused alike:

'We all of us further state that the whole time the Prisoner was in Court, he conducted himself in a most familiar manner, if not with absolute contempt, towards the Bench, without being reproved for so doing and, notwithstanding such conduct, the Magistrates' Clerk, Mr Bond, treated him with marked respect.'

Staggering as the mere volume of these depositions may be to our modern eyes, not to mention the circumlocution and formality of expression, one cannot but admire the sheer tenacity of purpose displayed — even though one may be left marvelling that Blockade officers had any time or energy left to pursue smugglers.

The Purser and the Pea-shooter

This is yet another illustration of the almost incredible thoroughness with which the Coast Blockade officers would investigate the slightest irregularity. The pedantic verbosity common to most official reports is also well demonstrated and the respect accorded by the lower echelons to their masters comes over most clearly.

The Purser of the 3rd Division of the Coast Blockade, one William Basden, was stationed in the army barracks at Shorncliffe, the training camp which, established near Folkestone some years previously, had produced the Light

Infantry which proved itself in the Peninsular War. Shorncliffe Camp is to this day very much in use.

It appears that Basden and the Barrack Master (an old officer veteran on half-pay acting as a kind of superior caretaker for the buildings) were at loggerheads. The Purser's jeremiad opens thus:

Shorncliffe Infantry Barracks 25th November 1825.
To: Lieutenant Samuel Hellard, * Superintending the Third Division of the Coast Blockade.*

Sir,

Finding that several unfounded and vexatious representations have been made by Mr Robert Metcalfe, the Barrack Master here, to the Honourable Board of Ordnance (*the Army organisation comparable to the Board of Admiralty*), reflecting on my conduct, which has tended to place me in an unfavourable point of view with that Board—and also, in a measure, to draw upon me their displeasure, as well as that of the Right Honorable the Lords Commissioners of the Admiralty, and having reason to believe that he, Mr Metcalfe, will continue to follow up the same line of conduct towards me, I feel myself reluctantly called on (in vindication of an irreproachable Character during upwards of Twenty Years Naval Service as a Purser) to represent to you, for the information of Captain Pigot (*the officer who had assumed command of the Eastern Division of the Blockade after McCulloch's death*) that since I have been Quartered in these Barracks (a period of nearly two years) I am not conscious of having in any one instance infringed or disobeyed any Order, or Regulation, of the Honourable Board made known to me; indeed, I have been scrupulously particular in the observance thereof, that no cause of complaint should be given, which I trust is manifest from Mr Metcalfe having been driven to the necessity of producing unfounded and frivolous subjects for complaint . . .

Mr Basden proceeds in this vein over the next three handwritten pages, enumerating his complaints and enlarging upon them. First was the matter of the Mess Kitchen, which Mr Metcalfe accused the Purser of using for his washing! Basden admits this, but adds in mitigation that he:

'begs to avow that no intimation was ever given me of such use being irregular . . . the result of Mr Metcalfe's accusation has been my *total exclusion* from the said Kitchen for Cooking'.

Next comes the Barrack Master's complaint of

'considerable damage having lately taken place in the Windows of the

*See Appendix A

unoccupied Barracks . . . the Persons having been intercepted in their improper Conduct last evening . . .'

Here, Mr Metcalfe plainly had a rod in pickle for the Purser's twelve-year-old son who had been seen in the vicinity holding a pea-shooter and being, so it was alleged,

'egged on by a female tutoress or domestic'.

Mr Basden thinks it far more likely that the damage was done by drunken soldiers; he knows for a fact that the Barracks Watchman, John Crowther, runs a sutling-room in his quarters

'where men are known to be frequently intoxicated'.

Adding insult to injury comes the case of the chickens, but however much one may sympathise with Mr Basden and his troubles with an over-officious neighbour, it is impossible to escape the feeling that here he really scrapes the bottom of the barrel:

'I feel utterly at a loss to conjecture the reason of Mr Metcalfe's hostile conduct towards me, never having to my knowledge given him any provocation on the contrary I have for some time past been the uncomplaining sufferer from the injury done to my Forage by the quantity of Poultry kept by him and Sergeant McDiarmid resorting to the Forage Barn, from which I find it impossible to keep them . . .'

Continuing that he has 'no wish to introduce any recriminatory matter', he proceeds to do exactly that with the complaint that 'the orders of the Honourable Board of Ordnance, while they have been enforced by Mr Metcalfe towards me, have been disregarded by himself.'

Lt Hellard, ordered to investigate the situation, set to with his customary thoroughness:

'Sir, in compliance with your memorandum of the 28th Ultimo, I have made strict enquiry into the circumstances complained of by the Barrack Master at Shorncliffe. I have to acquaint you that the lad alluded to was certainly playing near the quarters of the Barracks Master at the time in question with a pea-blower or tin tube, a plaything generally used by boys of that age, when by accident a single pea was blown from the tube which struck an upstair window a description of which I have placed in the margin, and the distance of the boy from the Glass being at least 21 feet, I should say that it could not have been broken or even cracked thereby . . . as the pea struck it in an oblique direction, in support of which I have looked at the window wherein it was stated that the two panes were broken and find the lower one *cracked* in the corner which from the situation of the lad could not have been done by him. The other pane, you will observe, was struck near the centre which is also *cracked* and I have not any hesitation in saying that from the appearance of the window under these circumstances the glass could not have been broken by Mr Basden's Son; as surely the force of a pea discharged merely by the breath of a lad at so great a distance and in such a direction could not at any rate have broken two panes . . .'

Mr Hellard then flies to protect the honour of the lady involved:

'The Barrack Master . . .. throws an impure slur on a young lady immediately under the protection of the officer in question . . . I have to observe that she is most respectably connected and is the daughter of a magistrate (*not, one imagines, on the Folkestone Bench, see p.85*) for whom Mr Basden can vouch as being the last to encourage a youth to commit such acts as the Barrack Master has thought unblushingly to charge her . . .'

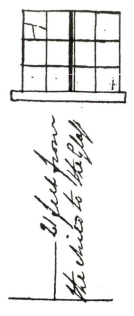

Lieut. Hellard's diagram of the cracked window.

This was by no means the end of the sniping. In that same year (1825), the Blockade Divisional Surgeon registered a strong complaint that a copper had been removed without his permission from his hospital kitchen, recently taken over from the Army. Once again, according to the Navy, the Barrack Master betrays a deplorable lack of good breeding:

'In what manner he gained access, I know not . . . I consider this an improper act . . . entering the apartments in so clandestine a way . . . leaves little doubt that there must have been other motives than that of repairing the copper which caused its removal . . .'

Some Clerical Criticism Contained

It was just after Christmas 1824 that the Rector of Selsey, the Reverend Burne Shipps — in the circumstances a wildly inappropriate name — complained to the Admiralty of 'the systematic non-attendance of the Blockade Service, both Officers and Men, at Church on the Sabbath'. Captain McCulloch utterly refutes this charge, demolishing it with characteristic thoroughness and, it has to be admitted, wordiness; it took him six pages of good Admiralty writing paper to scupper the unfortunate Rector. He wrote thus:

'Sir, in reply, I have the honour to acquaint you, for the information of My Lords Commissioners of the Admiralty, that, as the representation of the Reverend Rector is not true, it is possible that he refers to the 'whole' of the Blockade Service as being within his own Rectorial District, or that he has been misinformed . . .'

He proceeds to make several telling points in rebuttal of the charge; many officers and men do indeed attend church, but only

'where it can be done without giving the most evident advantages to the Smugglers.'

He admits that there are some churches on the coast which the men are forbidden to attend where

'there is insufficient accommodation for them without the necessity of their being separated from each other, in consequence of the Church having been made the chief resort of the Smugglers for the purpose of meeting and tampering with the men of this Service and . . . notwithstanding the vigilance of the Officers who accompany the Men to church, the Smugglers generally find means of supplying them with Liquor, when they frequently become drunk and riotous . . .'

Furthermore, McCulloch reasons, the vast majority of his seamen and petty officers are Roman Catholics and many Kent priests have approached him

'offering their services in attending the men in their religious duties.'

He has so far managed to put them off,

'not knowing to what effect their visits might tend'

but, if he allows the Protestants to attend church, how can he in all justice refuse the same privilege to the Roman Catholics. All these considerations apart, the fact must also be faced that, with the Blockade so weak in manpower, church-going of any description will give the smugglers more scope than ever and must therefore be ruled out. A face-saving compromise is finally suggested; since the Rector lives so near the Blockade stations within his parish, he will be most welcome to visit them and the Roman Catholics will be allowed similar facilities if they want them. Thus the

'considerable risk of giving the other Parishioners opportunities to land the usual supplies of genuine Port Wine and other Foreign luxuries with which they have hitherto been enabled to supply their Friends in ample abundance'

will be obviated. This was a judgement of Solomon which clearly convinced the Admiralty; a marginal annotation in a clerkly hand reads: *Their Lordships have received a satisfactory explanation on this subject from Capt McCulloch.*

'A Hard Fighter, of Reckless Courage'

This well merited compliment bestowed by Captain McCulloch upon Lieut. Peat for his conduct previously described (p.71) could have well been applied to most of the other Blockade officers; his career is typical of many.

His wounds having healed, Peat returned to Blockade duty. One spring night in 1821, patrolling the Marsh accompanied by QM Richard Wooldridge and two seamen, Robert Hunter and John Walker, they met up with a strong smuggling party whom they immediately challenged, detaining one of them. A volley split the Marsh stillness and Wooldridge fell dead; the rest of the patrol were hit and lay where they had fallen, feigning death and listening to the gang debate their next move over their inert bodies: 'That b...... Peat's got more lives than a cat! Let's give him another volley and finish him off! This they did, leaving all four sailors for dead. McCulloch later reported:

'Lieut Peat is most severely wounded and from head to foot riddled with musket balls and sluggs. Eight balls have already been extracted and he has received in all about twenty wounds. He suffers much . . . Walker and Hunter were wounded severely but are doing well . . . Wooldridge fell covered with wounds, two balls having passed through his lungs. This is the second time that Peat has been severely wounded in the gallant discharge of his duty within a very short time; he has been my chief support in all cases where courage and a steady conduct were particularly necessary. I am now deprived of his services, on which I could at all times rely, and I trust that I may be permitted to express my most anxious hope that my Lords Comms. of the Admiralty may consider him deserving of their favour and support . . .'

Peat did recover; he was promoted to Commander and was awarded a pension of £91.5.0 per annum but not only that — he 'later astonished the inhabitants of Folkestone by appearing at the theatre in his uniform'. Eventually he transferred to the Coast Guard at Hastings, achieving his Captaincy on 1st January 1847.

The Brookland Affray

The so-called Battle of Brookland marks the start of McCulloch's all-out campaign against the Aldington smugglers; it was to drag on over the six years following and, indeed, 'Flogging Joey' was to die without seeing his old enemy George Ransley brought to book.

In the dark of the early hours of Sunday, 11th February 1821, a strong body of smugglers made their stealthy way down to Camber beach, near Rye, to make ready to receive an incoming load of contraband. Suddenly, a single flash from the approaching vessel shone out in the gloom, to be seen by a Blockade sentry who fired a warning shot as was ordered. A party of seamen headed by four young officers, Digby*, James, Mckenzie and Newton*, came up at the double to intercept the gang. Too late to prevent the unloading, they pursued the tub carriers off the beach and harried them over the Marsh towards Brookland village firing volley after volley at them and making repeated cutlass charges. They were met with a return fire of considerable volume and accuracy from the covering fighting parties who 'behaved with the precision of trained soldiers' — as quite possibly some of them had been, not long since. McKenzie, badly wounded, lost contact with his men and wandered semi-conscious on the Marsh for some

*See Appendix A

hours until he was taken in by a cottager who conveyed him to that well-known smuggling rendezvous, the George Inn at Lydd. Here he lingered for two days; his burial is recorded in the Lydd parish register, but no memorial exists in the graveyard and it is thought that his family may have later arranged for his burial elsewhere. Digby, Newton and Jones fared better, although they were wounded, along with six of their men. The trio were commended to the Admiralty for their bravery and promoted forthwith to Lieutenant.

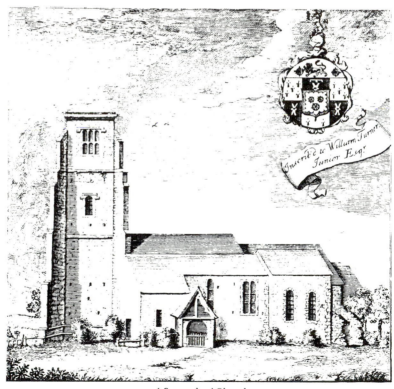

A Smugglers' Church
Cephas Quested buried here. (see page 97)
(Old print)

As to the smugglers, four were killed, a dozen wounded and two captured. Both of these were tried at the Old Bailey on 17th April 1821; the first, Richard Wraight put up a defence so ingenuous that it was almost insulting to the jury's intelligence. He swore that he had nothing to do with the smugglers, that he was in the battle area by pure mischance, having been out rook-shooting (this explained the powder traces on his face and hands) and that he had lost his way back home across the Marsh. Despite McCulloch's shrewd suspicion that he was the leader and notwithstanding the fact that, as a local man, it would have been very doubtful that he would have lost his way, his explanation was accepted and Wraight went free.

Not so with Cephas Quested however, for he had actually mistaken Newton for a smuggler (the officer was wearing a gaberdine smock) and had thrust a loaded musket into his hands saying 'Take this and blow some bloody officer's brains out.' This incitement was quite sufficient to hang him; although offered the chance to save his own skin by betraying his friends, he refused ('I've done wrong and I am prepared to suffer, but I won't bring harm on others') and was accordingly hanged in Newgate prison on 4th July 1821. His body was returned to his native Aldington, where it was buried in an unmarked grave.

Hastings defies the Blockade

Barely four weeks following the Brookland affair, the widespread bitter feelings against the Blockade were intensified at Hastings when a young fisherman was shot dead on the beach. The facts seem to have been stated fairly in a contemporary unofficial report:

'When a fleet of sixty fishing boats often lands in a single tide, it is impossible to undergo the labour of pulling out and re-stowing all the heavy nets, although it is well known that smuggled goods are very frequently concealed underneath. The Blockade sentinels are therefore furnished with sharp iron prickers to pierce through the nets, but this can not be done

97

A favourite spot near Hastings both for lovers and smugglers. (Fairlight Glen, old print)

without slightly damaging the nets and is generally considered unjustifiable by the fishermen. On one of these occasions, a man named England proceeded to examine the boat of John Swain, who declared that he would not have his nets injured by the pricker. As England persevered, a scuffle ensued in which England was thrown upon the beach. Irritated at this rough usage, he drew forth his pistol and shot poor Swain dead upon the spot. The sensation this caused in Hastings will not easily be forgotten; a furious mob surrounded England, who would probably have been dragged forth to his instant death, if a military guard had not been employed to intimidate the populace . . .'

The Blockade commander of the Hastings sector was Lieutenant Mark Sweeney, 'a cool and reliable officer'; he puts the episode in a rather different light:

'England got into the fishing-boat to search; the deceased resisted, striking him and throwing him out of the boat, following him and repeating the blow, forcing the cutlass out of his hand and flinging it into the sea. He then attempted to take from him his pistol, by which act he lost his life . . . By timely aid given by parties from Towers Nos 39, 42, 44, and 45, we were enabled to overawe the infuriated populace, in which we were aided promptly by the cavalry stationed here and at Bexhill . . .'

He concludes with an SOS to his commanding officer:

'The inhabitants threaten us with vengeance, and I much fear that without the most active interference by the magistrates, many lives will be lost . . . so circumstanced, I feel how much I stand in need of your instructions and, if your multifarious duties and health would admit, your presence.'

Whatever his shortcomings, McCulloch was never the man to withold support from his junior officers. Acting quickly and characteristically he made all possible speed for Hastings and promptly set up an inquiry to receive deputations from the fishermen and to hold discussions with the Mayor and the magistrates in some attempt to 'defuse the situation. He made an offer to remove the chief grievance — the irksome delay caused by the searches — by offering to detail six men (instead of one) to carry out the duty, but this suggestion was immediately countered by the objection that six was far too many men to allow on the boats. 'That,' as the Captain wearily observed, 'shows how unreasonable they are.' One can but sympathise with his complaint that 'the fishermen merely want an excuse for continuing their illicit practices.' England stood his trial for murder at Horsham on 28th March 1821 before a

Hastings—Fishermen's Quarters.
(Reproduced by kind permission of Ivan Green)

The tall black structures are the famous 'net shops'. These unique buildings are still used for storing nets and tackle; their design is said to be Elizabethan.

crowded courtroom. Nine Hastings fishermen swore that England deliberately walked round Swain, held the pistol six inches away from him and shot him; they were countered by five Blockade seamen on oath who declared that the firing was a pure accident 'arising from the suddenness of its release from the grasp of the accused, which caused the prisoner to stagger . . .' They denied that the prisoner took aim or that he walked around the fisherman; England's version of what happened tallied with theirs; his defence raised an objection in that the prosecuting council was Horsham's Coroner's Clerk and therefore bound to be prejudiced. The Judge summed-up in England's favour, pronouncing his conduct perfectly justified under the circumstances, but, 'so virulent was the rancour against the prisoner', the jury of twelve Sussex men good and true brought in their verdict of Guilty of Wilful Murder. A painful scene ensued with England 'bursting into violent grief . . . "My Lord, have mercy upon me! Consider, I was in the execution of my duty . . . Gentlemen of the jury, pray consider your verdict again!"' 'the death sentence was duly pronounced, but the elation of the Hastings smugglers was short-lived; England was granted an immediate free pardon and left the Blockade service forthwith. A memorial placed in All Saints Churchyard in the fisherman's quarter of Hastings kept John Swain's memory green:

'This Stone
Sacred to the Memory of
John Swain, Fisherman,
was erected at the Expence of
The Members of the Friendly
Society of Hastings
in Commiseration of his Cruel and Untimely Death,
and as a Record of the Public Indignation at the Needless
and Sanguinary Violence of which
He was the Unoffending Victim.
He was shot by Geo. England, one of the Sailors
Employ'd in the Coast Blockade service,
in open day, on the 15th March 1821,
And almost instantly expir'd, in the twenty-ninth year of his age,
leaving a Widow and five small Children
to lament his Loss.'

Smugglers and Fishermen—the roles were usually interchangeable.

Press Gang Sailors about 1790.

The Tragedy of Sydenham Snow

Hot on the heels of the Hastings incident came news of a serious affray at Herne Bay. Readers of the *Gentleman's Magazine* for May 1821 were appraised thus:

'An affray lately took place between a party of smugglers and the Preventive Service, immediately in front of the Ship Inn at Herne Bay. A large party of smugglers, in number reported from 100 to 150, came down from the interior of the country and, forming themselves into three divisions, one proceeded to unload a boat on the shore while the others posted themselves on the right and left, keeping up continued volleys from firearms, so as to prevent the approach of parties of the coast blockade stationed in the vicinity till the cargo of the boat (consisting, it is conjectured, of contraband articles packed in half-ankers) was conveyed away in carts brought in readiness for the purpose and guarded by those who accompanied them. At this moment, while the boat remained on the beach with her crew consisting of five or six men, Mr Snow, a midshipman of the *Severn*, belonging to the coast blockade, rushed forward and alone attempted to seize her when, being resisted, he pointed his pistol which missed fire; in consequence he was fired at by people in the boat and fell on the beach dangerously wounded, one ball having passed through his thigh

The scene of Midshipman Snow's Murder.
This photograph was taken at least 70 years ago, the inn would not have changed much since the old smuggling days. (Old Postcard)

103

and another through his shoulder, lodging under the blade-bone. After lying some time on the beach, he was conveyed to the Ship public-house, but with little expectation of recovery but, subsequently, the ball in the shoulder having been found, there are hopes of a more favourable issue'.

Unhappily, this optimism was not justified:

'Snow lingered on for a while in great agony, before he expired lamenting that his life had not been yielded in open battle with the enemies of his country instead of being sacrificed in a vile midnight encounter with a gang of outlaws'.

He was buried in Herne churchyard, a simple gravestone merely stating 'In Memory of Sydenham Snow, who died 21st April 1821 in the 24th year of his age'. Five smugglers, including an ex-petty officer of the Blockade, were tried at Bow Street for his murder. All were acquitted.

The End of the North Kents

Less than six months after Snow's death and heartened, no doubt, by the Bow Street verdict, the North Kent gang attempted a landing of goods from a six-oared galley at Marsh Bay, Margate. Midshipman Washington Carr and two seamen took on the entire hundred, most of whom were armed. Charging the party, they forced them to disperse; a musket and several bludgeons were abandoned. Although some were wounded, all the smugglers escaped, but one man had been identified; within twenty-four hours he was tracked down, arrested and turned King's evidence. James Bond, Bow Street runner, set to work and within a few months had collected sufficient evidence to warrant the arrest of eighteen suspects who subsequently made an appearance at Maidstone Spring Assize 1822. Daniel Baker, John Buffington, Francis Carden, Joseph Clements, Daniel Fagg, John Fagg, Joseph Gilbert, John Gill, Stephen Gummer, John Meredith, Thomas Mount, James Rolfe, Henry Smith, Thomas Stokes, Jas Taylor, Charles White, John Wilsden, Thomas Woollett were all charged with 'having feloniously assembled together, armed with fire-arms and other offensive weapons, in order to be aiding and assisting in the illegal landing and carrying away of uncustomed goods, and for having maliciously shot at and wounded Washington Carr, Thomas Cook and John Brimen, being in the execution of their duty as officers of the Coast Blockade.'

All were found guilty and sentenced to death; all save John Fagg, John Meredith, James Rolfe and John Wilsden escaped the gallows and were deported to Tasmania. The unlucky four were hanged on Penenden Heath, Maidstone on 4th April 1822 before a crowd estimated at 40,000; a Blockade officer who witnessed the executions afterwards wrote: 'The parting between these deluded men and their families was truly heart-rending.'

Hamilton's Ordeal

Relatively minor incidents were practically everyday happenings, but all were minutely and painstakingly recorded as the following account demonstrates; it also shows how difficult it could be to chase a smuggler, let alone catch one!

'Information of witnesses taken severally on behalf of our Sovereign Lord the King, touching the death of James Cunley at the dwellinghouse of William Holmes, known as *The Ship* in the parish of Dymchurch in the liberty of Romney Marsh on the twelfth day of June in the fourth year of the reign of our sovereign Lord George the Fourth &c &c before THOMAS DRAY, Esquire, one of the Coroners of the said Marsh on an Inquisition then and there taken on View of the Body of the said Jas Cunley then there lying dead as follows: Thomas Hamilton, Admiralty Midshipman belonging to HMS Ramillies stationed at No. 22 Tower . . . on his Oath saith that about half past 12 o'clock on this present day he was coming from the Circular Redoubt on the road parallel with Dymchurch Wall; he heard a noise apparently proceeding from a body of Men near to a Cottage and a stack of Faggots he proceeded to the spot accompanied by Samuel Everett, Seaman of HMS Ramillies, not finding any Person by the Faggot Stack he passed along the back of the Cottage and whilst in the act of crossing the railing near the House of Mr Dray, he observed a large Body of Men, about 40 or 50, apparently kneeling and certainly having long Guns in their hands. He hesitated a little, drew his sword and demanded to know who they were. Receiving no answer to his repeated question, he drew a Pistol and fired into the air as a signal for more assistance . . . upon this the Body of Men formed into a triangle and put their Guns into a position to fire. The Deponent took his Musquet from his Orderly and whilst he was doing so, the nearest Body of Men called out to the others, who seemed to be going off, "Come back,

The Scene of QM Morgan's Murder. (see page 107)　　(Old print)
'Within the town of Dover, near the bathing machines'.

CUSTOM HOUSE, LONDON.

1st August, 1826.

WHEREAS it has been represented to the Commissioners of his Majesty's Customs, that about one o'clock in the morning of the 30th ultimo, RICHARD MORGAN, a first-rate Quarter Master, and MICHAEL PICKETT, a Seaman, both belonging to the Service of the Coast Blockade for the Prevention of Smuggling, and stationed at the Casemates at Dover under the orders of Lieutenant Thomas S. Hall, were out on duty on the beach, and observed a boat in the surf, upon which the said RICHARD MORGAN fired his pistol as an alarm, when several smugglers, armed with long Duck Guns, stepped forward from the body of smugglers collected near the bathing machine, within the Town of Dover and fired at, and instantly killed the said RICHARD MORGAN; and with their fire-arms beat and wounded the Seaman RICHARD PICKETT; and that afterwards thirty-three tubs of Foreign Run Spirits were found and seized near the spot, and deposited in the Custom-House at Dover.

The said Commissioners are hereby pleased to offer a Reward of

FIVE HUNDRED POUNDS

to any Person or Persons who shall discover, or cause to be discovered any one or more of the said Offenders, so that he or they may be apprehended and dealt with according to Law, to be paid by the Collector of his Majesty's Customs at the Port of Dover, upon conviction.

By Order of the Commissioners,

T. WHITMORE, Secretary.

Announcement in Kentish Gazette, 18th August, 1826.

you Cowards, shoot again and we will give it to them." The Deponent then jumped over the railing, upon this the Men retreated to the rear of Mr Dray's premises, the Deponent pursuing them, but, being a stranger to the situation, lost sight of them. Owing to the paling which enclosed it, the Deponent experienced considerable difficulty in getting out of Mr Dray's garden . . . and found further difficulty in crossing the ditch behind it . . . he again caught sight of the Body of Men but, owing to the roughness of the ground, he fell and his Musquet went off . . .'

The Deposition continues by describing how Hamilton overtook one of the gang, the man begging him for mercy and beseeching him to assist another of the gang who was badly wounded. It continues:

'The Deponent then said "Direct me thither" which he did willingly; they returned towards the Sea about One hundred and fifty yards and found another man who said "I am shot, give me some water." The first man then said to the Deponent "Mr Hamilton, for God's sake send for a wattle *(Kentish dialect for a wicker hurdle used as portable fencing)* to carry the man to the nearest house, or the poor fellow will be dead." The Deponent's orderly then remarked "Sir, he calls you by name;" the Deponent replied: "I heard him, and mark that Circumstance," observing that he knew him to be a Folkestone man. After some little time, Mr Bambridge and Mr Gilson, midshipmen, came up with a party of seamen when they were enabled to carry the deceased to the front of the Cottage of Thomas Brown, where he expired before they could get admittance. And this Deponent further saith that he did not know of any Contraband goods having been worked then.'

Hamilton was arrested on a murder charge; after eleven uncomfortable days spent in the Dymchurch 'noggin' or lock-up, he was taken up to London for questioning and then sent for trial at Maidstone (7th August 1823) where he was honourably acquitted 'and had the satisfaction of being highly complimented by his judge, as well as by Captain McCulloch and the Blockade officers'. Further details of Hamilton's career are given in Appendix A.

Murder by the Bathing Machines

Perhaps the fate of the North Kents gave the Blues cause to ponder; whatever the reason, their activities practically ceased for more than a year while the Blockade continued to increase its strength. By the spring of 1826 there were close on 3,000 men on the books of *Ramillies* and *Hyperion*, about three

The Casemates today.

times as many as would have been the full complement for normal sea-going duties; the running costs of the Force for 1825 totalled £160,740.8.3.

A Report made to the Admiralty dated 14th March 1826 marks the end of the lull, setting the scene for an approaching storm:

'Armed parties of smugglers are again appearing on the coast within the limits of the Blockade . . . these public robbers belong to the parish of Aldington and are headed by George Ransley, a smuggler of notoriety in this neighbourhood'.

More, much more, was to follow, as Lieut Samuel Hellard of the Blockade reported from 'The Casemates, Dover' *(these were a part of the cliff fortifications, used as accommodation for the Blockade in much the same way as the Martello towers).*

'30th July 1826: Richard Morgan, who met with his death at about 1.00 a.m. near the bathing machines, was coming back from the Townsend Battery and when near the spot at which he met his death, he observed a boat in the surf and called out to Richard Pickett (Blockade seaman) "What boat is that?" Immediately he ran forward, when a party of smugglers armed with long duck-guns levelled their pieces at them and shot Morgan in the left side near the heart . . . Pickett also received several blows from the armed party with the butt ends of their muskets. A quantity of goods was got off clear, only 33 half-ankers being seized.'

Hellard continues his report complaining that

'the Casemates are difficult of ingress and egress, being so far up the cliff'

and points out that several successful 'runs' have been made at the spot for this reason. Later that same day, Hellard dashed off a further report:

'There are a number of strangers of the lower orders at this moment in the town of Dover and I submit to you, Sir, the propriety of having one or two of the most active officers from Bow Street immediately sent to this town, which I am firmly convinced would secure the arrest of someone of this lawless party.

More Mayhem at Hythe

Six days later, elated by success and never doubting the quality of Ransley's leadership, the Blues came out in strength at Fort Moncrieff, near Hythe. Lieut Johnstone was patrolling the beach in the early hours of 6th August; seeing two flashes out at sea, followed by the sound of oars and pistol shot, he ran forward towards the noise, accompanied by three seamen, to find a large galley just beached and being unloaded by smugglers. The Blockade patrol opened fire, dropping three, one of whom Johnstone grabbed. A violent struggle ensued with the gang leader shouting 'Kill the bastards!' With the further exchange of shots, the smugglers retreated, leaving behind one man wounded in the right knee, who gave his name as James Bushell. Fourteen tubs of spirits were recovered and at this juncture another Blockade squad arrived and pursued the gang deep into the Marsh where three muskets and one empty tub were later recovered —

'the tub, being shot through the bilge, it is fair to calculate that the man who carried it is either dead or wounded.'

Hellard, who made the report, continues:

'James Bushell was wounded in the right knee, rendering amputation necessary. His present position prevents the possibility of my getting any particulars from him, except that the party assembled in the village of Alkham, about four miles from Folkestone, and that he belongs to the parish of Hawkinge, commonly called Ackinge, the adjoining parish to Alkham. I hope in a day or two to get some good information from him, as he appears to be communicative. . .'

George Ransley's Cottage, the Bourne Tap, Aldington Frith, as its stands today.
(Author's photograph)

Spreading the Net

Report from J. Smith, Bow Street Officer

'The Packet Boat Inn, Dover, 7th August 1826. The smuggler taken at Brookman's Barn, Hythe, last Sat. night, says his name to be Jas Bushell, but I think he will turn out to be Jas Quested, who had a brother or some such relative hung at Newgate some time since *(Cephas Quested, see p. 97)* . . . I have no doubt but that he was with them that shot Morgan at Dover . . . Capt. P(igot)* and Lieut H(ellard) are desirous that I should bring M(arsh)** to London. The prisoner in the meanwhile will when able be brought round to Deal and put on board the Ramillies & thence to London. Your obed't servant, J. J. Smith.'

*the officer who took over McCulloch's command on his death in 1825.
**extract from Pigot's report to the Admiralty: "A person named William Marsh has offered to give information . . . it appears to me that through this quarter several of the offenders may be brought to justice . . . I have found it expedient to authorize Wm Marsh to be supplied with a small amount of money for subsistence . . ."

Poster exhibited in Dover

'WHEREAS it has been represented to the Commissioners of HM Customs that at about one o'clock in the morning of the 30th ultimo, RICHARD MORGAN, a First-rate Quartermaster and MICHAEL PICKETT, a Seaman, both belonging to the Service of the Coast Blockade for the Prevention of Smuggling . . . were out on duty on the beach and observed a boat in the surf, upon which the said RICHARD MORGAN fired his pistol as an alarm, when several smugglers, armed with long duck-guns . . . fired at & instantly killed the said RICHARD MORGAN . . . the said Commissioners are hereby pleased to offer a Reward of FIVE HUNDRED POUNDS to any Person or Persons who shall discover . . . any one or more of the said Offenders, so that he or they may be apprehended and dealt with according to Law . . .'

Extract from the *Kentish Chronicle* 29th October, 1826

'Murder of Morgan. This morning (18th October) intelligence was brought to Dover that one of the party concerned in the murder of Morgan of the Coast Blockade, who was a short time ago shot by a band of smugglers in front of the Marine Parade, had made disclosures implicating, some say twenty, and others thirty, in the barbarous action. A reward of £1,000 *(note the discrepancy with the sum offered in the Custom House poster)* was offered for their apprehension at the time, and the reward is said to have prompted the informer, an inhabitant of Deal, to come forward voluntarily and give information.'

The Trap is Sprung . . .

'I have the honour to inform you that, warrants having been obtained against the parties implicated in the murder of Richard Morgan, the same were entrusted to Lieut Hellard, superintending the Right Division, assisted by two officers from Bow Street. I now have much pleasure in communicating with you that Lieut Hellard has succeeded in arresting George Ransley and seven of his gang . . .'

(Captain Hugh Pigot, reporting to the Admiralty 18th October 1826)

Let Samuel Hellard tell the story his own way:

'I have the honour to acquaint you that, in obedience to your orders, I last night at 11.00 p.m. proceeded with a party of officers and sentries from Fort Moncrieff accompanied by police officers Bishop and Smith. Having marched in the direction of Aldington reached that place at about 3.00 a.m.

111

this morning . . . every house in which I expected to arrest a man was surrounded by sentinels nearly at the same moment. I then instantly advanced to the dwelling of George Ransley the leader of this ruffian band, and was fortunate enough to get so close to his house before his dogs were disturbed that he had not time to leave his bed; the dogs were cut down and his door forced; when I rushed in, I had the statisfaction to seize the man in his bedroom. Having handcuffed him to one of the stoutest men in the party, I proceeded to the other houses and was equally successful in arresting seven others of the gang, whose names I subjoin. On my return to Fort Moncrieff at 8.00 a.m., I immediately embarked the prisoners on board the *Industry* for a passage to *Ramillies* where I presume they will arrive as soon as this reaches Deal. Before I conclude this report, I consider it a most particular part of my duty to inform you that the conduct of the officers and men under my direction on this service was most exemplary throughout the night and during a most fatiguing march of nearly thirty miles . . .'

(Lieut Hellard's Report to Capt Pigot, 17 October 1826.)

'No time was lost in bringing the prisoners before the Bow Street examining magistrate, Sir Richard Birnie. Sir Richard was an interesting character, a walking example of the 19th century "rags to riches" success story. The son of a Banff saddler, he arrived as a boy in London, friendless and penniless. He obtained work with the royal harness-makers, was promoted foreman and later a partner, attracting the attention of the Prince Regent. His actions as a magistrate were described as "energetic, courageous and intrepid"'.

A contemporary newspaper describes this particular occasion:.

'Considerable interest was excited at Bow Street on Friday morning October 27th in consequence of the news having been circulated that a desperate gang of smugglers had been apprehended in the county of Kent and would be brought up for examination. At about half-past twelve, George Ransley, Samuel Bailey, Robert Bailey, Richard Wire, William Wire, Thomas Gillian, Charles Giles and Thomas Denard, all men of fierce aspect, were brought to the office and charged with the wilful murder of Richard Morgan . . . the prisoners were all dressed in smock-frocks with the exception of Ransley, the captain of the gang, who was a very fine looking man, apparently possessing great muscular strength.'

Despite representations by the smugglers' lawyer, the wily Mr Platt of Ashford ('a gentleman associated with most of the smuggling cases of those days'), the Examining Magistrate decided that there was a case to answer and so, with Mr Platt advising them to say nothing for the moment, the prisoners were committed for trial and remanded in Newgate prison, it being thought necessary 'to confine them in a place of more security than any provided on the Kent coast; it was a notorious fact that smugglers had broken open or pulled down every prison in their part of the country . . .' Furthermore, as it was also pointed out, a certain difficulty existed in inducing the Cinque Port magistrates to back warrants against smugglers as they themselves were often not unconnected with the Trade.

... but the Gallows are cheated

Sharp at 9.00 a.m. on Friday 12th January 1827 the trial opened at Maidstone,

'some time before the opening of the Court, the doors were beseiged by a great number of people anxious to hear the trial . . . Mr Justice Park took his seat on the Bench and the Court was instantly filled in every part . . .' *(Kentish Chronicle)*.

The nineteen year-old Richard Wire was charged with the actual murder, the others with assisting him. All pleaded Not Guilty; after lengthy discussion between counsels for both sides, further lesser, but still capital, charges were brought of smuggling and shooting at Revenue officers. To these, all pleaded guilty. The *Chronicle* continues:

'The Solicitor-General then stated that the prisoners having pleaded Guilty to other charges by which they forfeited their lives to the laws of the country, it was not his intention to offer any evidence against them on the charge of murder. He could not say that their lives would be spared but, as far as his recommendation would go, they should have the benefit of it; at all events they would most probably be sent out ot the country for the rest of their lives. By this merciful arrangement *(the possible reasons for this are discussed in 'Smuggling-The Wicked Trade')* two of the prisoners (Robert Bailey and Thomas Wheeler) are wholly acquitted, they having been indicted for the murder only . . . Mr Justice Park then addressed the remaining prisoners, saying that they had pleaded Guilty to a most heinous offence, the commission of which struck terror into every well-disposed mind. They assembled in numerous bodies to aid in the running of uncustomed goods . . . they had fired upon persons only doing their duty . . . it must be known throughout the country that if an offence of this nature were again committed, no mercy would be shewn to the offenders . . . if persons in the highest stations in life were not to purchase smuggled goods, there would be an end to smuggling, but many laboured under the delusion that defrauding the revenue was no crime . . . His Lordship then passed sentence of Death in the usual form. The Calendar states that the smugglers are to be executed on 5th February but it is not expected that any of them will suffer.'

This prediction was confirmed in the *Kentish Times* of 9th February:

'On Thursday morning last, Mr Agar, Governor of the County Gaol Maidstone received a letter from the Secretary of State, signifying that the execution of the sentence of death passed upon the smugglers at the East Kent Assizes should be respited until the further significance of His Majesty's pleasure. Agreeable to the further orders, all fourteen prisoners were removed from the gaol to be put on board ship for transportation for life . . .'

So fell the curtain on one of Kent's most sensational trials of the century; this was the last time that a smuggling gang would be tried for taking up arms against the King's officers.

Stood Down—Paid Off

'On Friday last, five men apprehended in a smuggling transaction at Shellness by Lieut Autridge underwent an examination before the Revd Dr Poore & W. Lushington Esq (magistrates) at the Dover Castle Inn, Green Street. All being young and able they were sentenced to serve five years in the Navy; their names being Thomas Brown, James Hall, Richard Keen, Henry Coltrup and Thomas Wood. They were all escorted to Green Street and guarded by a party of the Coast Blockade who had strict orders to be watchful of the prisoners. Notwithstanding this precaution, one of them, Thomas Wood, actually walked away unobserved by the guard and regained his liberty, to the infinite joy of the bystanders . . .' (*Kentish Gazette* 12th Oct 1830).

With the Aldington gang safely put away, the Blockade's decline accelerated and instances of slackness became more and more frequent. Moral and *esprit de corps*, perhaps never of the highest, sank lower still to reach its nadir when several men in *Hyperion* resorted to self-mutilation in an attempt to obtain their discharge.

At least one officer tried to 'work his ticket', as recalled by Captain J. Boteler RN:

'I left the coach at Bexhill and walked down to the beach to look for Paddy Norcott who was in a (Martello) tower not far off . . . I was received most heartily, as also by his wife, who at once exclaimed "Oh, Mr Boteler, aren't you surprised to see me here?" I have only two antipathies in the world—rats and a step-ladder—and when I got out of the carriage there they were before me. I thought I should have fainted! But Paddy was greatly excited and offered to set me up with every possible thing I might want &c, &c. I spent an agreeable hour in the tower . . . He is much disgusted with his quarters and the Service and more so with Captain Mingaye* *(commander of the Western Division of the Blockade)* who in no way would let him leave . . . Two or three months later, when in Portsmouth harbour, I saw *Hyperion's* tender, the cutter *Wolf*, coming in. With the aid of my glass, I made out Norcott on deck; I was soon alongside and could not help laughing, he had on a white cap and an old glazed cocked hat over it. "Why, what's the matter, Norcott?" "Oh, I am not at all well, I am going to the hospital to be invalided." He said this with a grave face, but with a twinkle in his eye; I continued to stare at his very white face. At last, he laughed out, "I have chalked my face, I hope Dr Mortimer won't see it, I don't know how it will end, I mean to chalk my tongue a little before I show it." Some days after, I called on him at Haslar he told me that Dr Mortimer, after feeling his pulse and looking at his tongue, asked what ailed him and on his reply that the tower was damp and gave him colds and rheumatic pains and that the coastguard service *(Capt Boteler must have meant the Blockade)* disagreed with him. "Ah," said the doctor, once more peering into his face, "I see, I see," smiling, "But we must try to set you up" . . . All the medicine given Paddy went out of the window, he shewed me where it trickled down a lean-to roof. He was very comfortably lodged, though only for a time, for all ended in his being invalided.'

*See Appendix A

More contraband was to be run, more blood was to be shed on our south-eastern shore, but the end, as far as the Blockade was concerned, was nigh. By January 1830, the Kent shore patrols were cut by 350 men and in the year that followed all the auxiliary vessels were paid-off, soon to be followed by *Talavera* 74 (she having replaced *Ramillies* some three years previously) and *Hyperion*. It is noteworthy that the Navy List for March 1831 shows both these vessels still carrying no less than 65 lieutenants and 15 assistant surgeons each; the normal establishment would have been six of the former and three of the latter.

The demise of the Blockade does not appear to have upset the locals at all:

'The Coast Blockade, it is understood, will be abolished in April, the Coast Guard preparing to occupy the several stations. This measure is the reverse of that calculated to excite regrets in this part of the Sussex district' (*Sussex Advertiser* 21st March 1831) . . . 'The Coast Guard establishment under the new regulations of the Customs has commenced its duties within the last fortnight at Hastings; on Thursday twelve of the horse-police arrived for the interior duty of the prevention of smuggling; they are rather well-looking men . . .' (*Ibid 4th April 1831*).

There was at least one Customs man who did not approve of the Blockade and did not mince his words:

'It admitted of more smuggling annually on the shores of the two counties committed to its charge than has occurred in the whole of the United Kingdom in the seven years subsequent to its abolition. Instead of being a nursery for seamen, it was no more than a temporary refuge for the outcasts of Society . . . For my part, if I were to throw overboard the good of the public revenue, I should at once say, "Give me the Blockade in preference to the Coast Guard." *(S. Price-Edwards, Yarmouth, 1839.)*

'Flogging Joey's' signature suggests self-confidence and tenacity of purpose. Note that only the actual signature is his, the rest would have been copied down by his writer (naval clerk) or someone, possibly the Purser, acting as his secretary.

These highly subjective observations must be qualified by the writer's own admission that

'I have not the means at hand to bring more forcibly into view the many defects of the Coast Blockade . . .'

A harsh judgment which in all fairness must be balanced by a more charitable view:

'In a time of grave national emergency when no other disciplined force was available, the services of 'the Handyman' were invoked in aid of the Civil Power and a large force of Naval officers and seamen actively and continuously employed on shore for a period of fifteen years in the capacity of Coast Police. Although called on to perform duties of a most vexing, dangerous and harassing nature, neither the civil authorities nor even the magistracy could be relied upon for support or even sympathy. Both officers and men, by reason of their duties interfering with the means of livelihood of the seaboard populace, were regarded with the bitterest animosity and subjected to the grossest calumnies and abuse; they were in frequent conflict with smugglers—fierce and reckless desperadoes of the worst type, they were liable to be shot at and brutally ill-treated and were not seldom murdered by unknown foes . . . and finally, the Coast Blockade having fulfilled its mission, the men—as, alas: too often happens in John Bull's service—were sent about their business without a word of acknowledgement from the authorities, or even a valedictory sermon. History, Naval or Civil, may be searched in vain for even an allusion to the Force.'

This contemporary glass painting depicts the capture by HMS *Shannon* of the U S Navy frigate *Chesapeake* outside Boston (1st June, 1803). The action took exactly 15 minutes but casualties on both sides were heavy, including *Shannon's* bosun who, in attempting to bind the two ships together, had his arm cut off. (see page 154)

Appendix A—The Men

Edward Digby

The second son of the Revd John Digby of Osberstown, Co Kildare and New Park, Co Leith and related to Captains Joseph Digby and Digby Marsh, he was born 14th April 1799 and entered as a Volunteer (6th August 1831) in *Devonshire* 74, thence as Midshipman to *Harlequin* 18 where, off Newfoundland, he assisted in the capture of the privateer *Ida* and was also present at 'a mistaken and very severe engagement' with the royal packet *Princess Charlotte*. The French wars ended, he served nearly four years in *Podargus* 16 guarding Napoleon on St Helena. Having passed his Lieutenant's examination, he was appointed to the Coast Blockade, earning promotion by his distinguished behaviour in the affray at Brookland. Transferring in 1826 to the Customs, he was appointed Inspector at Deal where, two years later, he was injured during an encounter with smugglers. He married Sarah, daughter of Hugh Crawford of Orangefield, Co Down, by whom he had a son and a daughter.

Richard Gardiner

I am greatly indebted to Mr John Fone of Norwich who, in reply to my request in the Kent Family History Society's Journal, kindly supplied much of this information on the life of his great-grandfather.

Born, according to Naval records, in Norwich, although family tradition says 'somewhere in India', it is nevertheless certain that some at least of his early days were spent in the East for it is in Calcutta at the age of 25 we find him

The name of DIGBY still stands high in Thanet. (see page 118)
Modern inn sign at Kingsgate
(Author's photograph)

volunteering for the Royal Navy. Entered as Landsman on the books of *Psyche* 36, a captured French vessel, he stayed with her on trooping and prize escort duty until she was condemned as unfit for further service. Thereupon, Gardiner was transferred to *Belliquex* 64 and made for Chatham, having in the meantime been twice promoted (to Ordinary Seaman July 1807 and to Able Seaman November 1808). After one year in *Belliquex* the entire company transferred to *Warrior* 74, a third-rater, to see action against the Danes (22nd July 1813) and to make a West Indies trip, during which they ran into a gale, the ship dismasted and several guns perforce jettisoned. Back in Chatham, *Warrior* too was condemned and Richard was discharged with the rating of Quartermaster. For the next ten years he forsook the sea and from September 1817 was employed in the Chatham Dockyard Ropery; meanwhile, he married a local girl, raising a family of four, two boys and two

Old photograph of St Mary's, Walmer.

At least two Blockade Officers were buried here:

Sacred to the Memory of
GODFREY SPRINGALL FINCH
Late Master's Mate of HMS *Severn*
who departed this life April 14th, 1823 Aged 29 years

JAMES NICOL
Native of Arbroath NB and
late Assistant Surgeon of HMS *Severn*
Zealous in the discharge of his Professional Duties
He fell a victim thereto by the accidental
Puncture of his Finger
June 17th 1820
Aged 27 years

girls. Both boys were destined to be lost at sea. Tiring, perhaps of humdrum ropemaking, Richard re-enlisted in *Glasgow* 50 as an AB in early 1825; soon he was off and away again to the West Indies. Within six months, he was made Ship's Corporal* and, returning the following year to Chatham, began his Blockade service as a Quartermaster in *Ramillies*. *(An added inducement to serve in the Blockade was that those in receipt of pensions were entitled to retain them on entering the Service. Had they re-entered an ordinary vessel, the pension would have been withdrawn.)* Reduced, for some reason so far not discovered, to AB in 1829, he quit the Navy once again—but only for two years for, on 11th May 1831, he rejoined (*Talavera* 74) his final two years being spent as Cook** on *Cambridge* 50. Richard Gardiner's last years were spent in the Royal Hospital, Greenwich, where he died in 1834.

Thomas Hamilton

Entered the Service as an AB—aged ten! This was a regulation-dodging device employed by some Captains enabling them to take on more than the officially entitled

In all those ships which did not carry Marines, a master-at-arms was expected to post sentinels and instruct them in their duty. He was assisted by two ship's corporals . . . who had the privilege of sleeping near the ship's side with rather more space than their shipmates . . . In day time they pried up and down in search of delinquents, whom they might thrash with their rattans (canes) or drag to the bilboes (iron bars fitted with sliding manacles) . . . the job was not popular for the increase in pay was slight, the responsibility heavy and the duty unpleasant . . . (Sea Life in Nelson's Time, Masefield J.)

**An important member of the ship's crew was the Cook. This warrant officer was appointed by the Commissioners of the Navy . . . he was seldom blessed with all his limbs and never rose beyond the making of pea-soup and the boiling of junk (salt meat)—'The composing of a minc'd Pye is metaphysics to him'—his Art was of the Popular kind—anyone could understand it. (Ibid)*

NB Out of respect for Richard Gardiner's memory and with deference to his descendants' feelings, I should point out that this book although very entertaining, is not always accurate and is decidedly biased! JAD quota of protégés; the correct rating would have been Volunteer or Boy 1st Class. After much action in *Barbara* 18 in the Channel and the Baltic, including several 'cutting-out' expeditions he took part in the New Orleans campaign (1812) and after some years' service joined the Coast Blockade in *Severn*; in one affray with the smugglers he was so badly injured — one arm fractured, lower jaw fractured, wounds to left eye and breast, three sabre cuts to the head — that he was given up for dead. Happily surviving, he was promoted Lieutenant and served in the Coast Guard many years thereafter.

Samuel Hellard

'A terrible man for cursing and swearing at his men' he entered the Navy as a Volunteer, 7th September 1798, in *Director* 64 under Capt Wm Bligh of *Bounty* fame. After one trip to the West Indies, he transferred to *Gladiator* 44 at Portsmouth, thence to *Blenheim* 74 in 1802. Returning the year following to the West Indies under Admiral Hood, he assisted at the 'cutting-out' of *Hermione*, a notorious privateer, at Martinique. Spring 1805 saw him as Midshipman in *Flora* 36, present at the capture at Oporto of the Spanish privateer *El Espedarte*. Shipwrecked off Holland (19th January 1808), he survived to join *Majestic* 74, the flagship of Vice Admiral Thomas Macnamara Russell in the North Sea. In *Castor* 32 as Master's Mate, he participated in the capture of *D'Hapoult* 74 (17th April 1808) and, as acting Lieutenant in the following December, was present at the sinking of the *Loire* 40 and the *Seine* 40, French store-ships protected by the Guadeloupe shore batteries; he commanded a shore party at the town's subsequent reduction in 1810. Confirmed in his lieutenancy, he joined *Podargus* 74 and shared in the capture and destruction of an entire Danish squadron off the Norwegian coast in July 1812. Further service in *Benbow* 74 and *Scout* 14 both at home and in the West Indies was followed by a transfer to the Coast Blockade, first in *Severn* (31st October-31st November 1823), thence to *Ramillies*, with a brief respite from the Kent smugglers (April-December 1824) in *Dover* 44 at Leith. His Blockade service finishing in *Talavera*, he continued with the Coast Guard and was promoted Captain on 1st January 1839. He subsequently retired on half-pay and is said to have died from typhoid in Ireland while supervising famine relief.

St Michael's Church, Newhaven 'refurbished and enlarged' with the help of the Coast Blockade. (Old Postcard)

Whatever the exigencies of the situation, Captain Mingaye and *Hyperion's* company did not spend all their time chasing smugglers; (see page 124) this much is obvious from an Agreement, signed by the Rector, Churchwardens and ten parishioners of the newly refurbished and enlarged Newhaven Parish Church granting the right 'as far as the power with which we are invested authorises us' for fifty seamen and marines to occupy free seats in the restored North Gallery. This was in recognition of 'the liberal aid afforded us in the erection of the said Gallery by the employment of Five Carpenters to assist in the Work'. It was noted the 'the Captain and Officers . . . are to pay at the rate of £5 per annum each for the Rent of Two Pews erected for their accommodation in the said Gallery'.

William James Mingaye

Entering the Navy as a Volunteer (16 September 1799) in *Anson* 6, he was present at the defeat of the French squadron carrying troops to Ireland and at the capture of *La Gloire* 46. After attending upon the King at Weymouth, he joined *Endymion* 40 in February 1801, assisting in the taking of a French privateer and escorting a whaling fleet home from St Helena. Wrecked off Brest (March 1804) in *Magnificent* 74 he joined the gun-brig *Tickler* 12 off Boulogne and remained in her until promoted Lieutenant, then transferring to *Brilliant* 64, serving ashore with the Naval brigade at the taking of the Cape of Good Hope in June 1806. After some years' service on the East Indies and Mediterranean stations, he returned to home waters joining the yacht *Royal George* and subsequently *Eridanus* 36. With promotion to Commander (2nd October 1817), he captained *Cameleon* 10 on the Portsmouth station; advanced to Post-Captain he attained acting command of *Royal George*, thence to *Romney* 50 newly fitting-out at Chatham in July 1824. Only six months later, perhaps due to the urgency of the smuggling situation, he was posted to command the Western (Sussex) Division of the Coast Blockade in *Hyperion* 40, lying at Newhaven. Six years after the Blockade's disbandment, Capt. Mingaye was still concerned with Newhaven's future. Writing (April 1837) in the *Sussex Agricultural Express* he underlines the town's potential:

'I should now say, accomplish a Railroad; and for vessels in the Fruit Trade, whose cargoes are intended for the London market, I know of no harbour better placed . . . if a Railway be constructed which will bring it within two hours and a half distance from London, *it must become of the greatest national importance.*'

Charles James Franklin Newton

Entering as a Volunteer (age 12) in *Egmont* 74 on 4th March 1812, he was employed at the blockades of Flushing, Texel and Cherbourg and also cruised in the Western Isles. In December 1813, he joined *Niger* 38, visiting the Cape of Good Hope, Brazil and the African coast, assisting in the capture of

Ceres 40 off Cape Verde (6th January 1814). The next year, he removed to *Vengeur* 74 at Portsmouth, thence to *Pelican* 16, *Ganymede* 20 and *Severn* 50, the last two vessels being part of the Coast Blockade in which he served with distinction, especially in the Brookland affray for which he was awarded his Lieutenancy; in that same year he was presented with a Sword of Honour by Lloyd's for life-saving off Dungeness. He left the Blockade in September 1821 on appointment to *Brisk* 10 on the Home station; three years later he commanded the bomb-ketch *Infernal* 6, and demonstrated the action of a rocket-boat before the Dey of Algiers. He was posted to *Prince Regent* 120, the Chatham flagship, in 1826 and stayed in her for three years, followed by a further two on another flagship, *Spartlaye* 74, thence to *Dublin* 50 both on the South America station. Promotion to Commander came on his return to England in June 1838; he served six years in the Coast Guard and then returned to the Navy to command *Lily* 16 off the African coast. In 1830 he married the only daughter of D. H. Day Esq, of Wilmington Hall, Dartford, Kent, by whom he had two children.

Dennis O'Mainnin (anglicised Manning)

This account is largely based upon information gathered by Manning's great-great-grandson, Mr Peter Manning of London, to whom I wrote after reading his article 'A Stepney Sailor's Family' in 'Cockney Ancestor' (the journal of the East London Family History Society). I am pleased to acknowledge Mr Manning's considerable and kind assistance.

Captain W. Glascock RN, writing at the time when the Blockade was in full swing, states categorically that the majority of its men (as opposed to officers) were 'unskilled, though hardy, Irish landsmen' and this fits Mr Manning's description of his ancestor's background exactly:

'Dennis O'Mainnin was born of a large, poor Irish Catholic farming family in 1798, in the parish of Kilbride, Co Roscommon. His family probably lived, as was usual, in a one-room cabin of mud and earth sods, the first two or three feet being of stone without mortar and roofed with branches and potato stalks covered with turves and thatched with straw and rushes'.

Having worked as a farm labourer, Dennis came to England as a young man by cargo ship, most probably to find work in the hay and corn harvests of the south; by the age of 26, he had gravitated to East London to join the Irish 'colony' at Wapping where many were employed digging the London and St Katherine's Docks.

He joined the Royal Navy as a Volunteer on 28th April 1825, being entered as a 'supernumerary seaman for the Coast Blockade' on the books of *Perseus* 22, a guard-ship lying off the Tower which sent out daily recruiting parties for the Navy, the press-gang having long gone out of business. Then it was that his name was put into its English form; from that day on he was to remain 'Manning'. After a few days instruction in basic seamanship from *Perseus'* bos'un, the recruits were taken down-river to the flagship *Prince Regent* 120 lying in the Medway off Folly Point. From there, the cutter *Surly* made the trip down-Channel to *Hyperion* the HQ ship of the Western Division of the Coast Blockade under Captain W. J. Mingaye, stationed at Newhaven. Now rated Landsman, Dennis was posted to Camber Watch-house at Rye along with forty other Blockadesmen. After a year's satisfactory service he was promoted to Ordinary Seaman and his pay rose from 10 d. to 11½ d. per day.

His three year engagement concluded, Dennis took his discharge and collected his back pay at Portsmouth. He then made his way back to Stepney to find work in the Docks, marrying a sailor's daughter and settling in Wapping, where their four children were born. Now employed as a ballast heaver unloading gravel and shingle off lighters, he was struck by sudden misfortune when he developed paralysis in both legs (1842). He applied for a place as an in-pensioner at the Royal Hospital Greenwich; within a fortnight he was admitted and lived out the rest of his days there, to die seventeen years later on 29th August 1859.

Hugh Pigot

A relative of Lt Gen Sir Robert Pigot (who commanded the left wing of the British Army at the Battle of Bunker's Hill in the American War of Independence), he started his Naval career on 1st May 1788 in *Salisbury* 50, later that year removing to the sloop *Merlin* and thence to *Southampton* 32, wherein he passed three years as midshipman. In 1792 he sailed for the Mediterranean in *Romney* 50, flag-ship of Rear-Admiral Sir Samuel Cranston Goodall, whom he accompanied in May 1793 to *Princess Royal* 93; further service in *Britannia* 100 saw him promoted Lieutenant whereupon he was posted to the sloop *La Fleche*. Following employment in *Gladiator* 44, *Surprise* 32, *Monarch* 74 and *Aeolus* 32 on the Mediterranean, Newfoundland, North Sea, Baltic and Jamaica stations, appointment to Commander of the sloop *Speedy* found him cruising off Seaford (Sussex) in August 1803. Less than a year later with the command of *Circe* 32 came his Post Captaincy and it was with this ship that he captured *L'Austerl* a French privateer and in the following year annexed the French West Indian island Marie-Galante on behalf of the British government, proceeding then to capture the brig *Galineur* off Martinique with the loss of only two men. In 1809, commanding the squadron blockading Guadeloupe in *Latona* 38, he participated in the taking of *La Junon* with minimum casualties (six wounded, none killed). For his action he was warmly thanked for 'his exertions and his ability in putting the prize into a sea-worthy state'. Similarly commended some two months later for 'his spirited exertions' during the pursuit and eventual capture of *D'Hapoult* 74, he shortly after took *La Félicité* complete with a valuable cargo of sugar and coffee. During the war with USA (1812-15) he sank two privateers and captured the *Frolic* 22 on 22nd April 1814. With the death of Captain W. McCulloch in October 1825, he assumed command of the Eastern (Kent) Division of the Coast Blockade in *Ramillies* 74, later transferring his command to *Talavera* 74 in September 1829. On the disbanding of the

Coast Blockade, he moved to command *Barham* 50 and later that year (1831) was created Commander of the Order of the Bath. After three years in the Mediterranean he was knighted and promoted Rear-Admiral in 1837; a further ten years saw him Vice-Admiral. From 16th May 1844 to 1st July 1847 he was C-in-C on the Cork station.

The headquarters of the Aldington gang.
(Photograph taken circa. 1900, Folkestone Library collection.)

128

A List of the Supernumerary Lieutenants of the Blockade who elected to stay on to serve with the Coast Guard.

These officers were carried on the books of one of the Blockade HQ vessels (either *Hyperion* or *Talavera*) at the time of the disbandment (April 1831). This was an administrative device for pay and other purposes; most would have been stationed ashore.

Name	Blockade Station	Coast Guard Station to which first posted
ASBY William	Littlehampton	Martello No. 62
BAKER Gustavus S.	Martello No. 24	Martello No. 24
BAKER William H.	—	—
BATE John Mort	—	St. Nicholas
BATT Henry	Shorncliffe	Shorncliffe
BATT William	—	Epple Bay
BECKETT William	—	Fort Sutherland
BENSON R.	—	Cornhill
BLISSET Charles E.	Lydden Spout	Lydden Spout
BOWDEN John	Birling Gap	Birling Gap
BROKENSHA Samuel	Folkestone	Newgate
CAREY Thomas	—	—
CARR Henry J.	—	—
CASWELL Thomas	Jury's Gap	—
CHAPPELL Edward	Bexhill*	—
COLLINS Francis	—	Martello No. 55
CONSUIT John	Winchelsea	Winchelsea
CONNOR Samuel	Hastings	Fairlight
COURTNEY Henry	Galley Hill	—
COWEN Morrice	Newhaven	—
CRISPO W.	Bearshide	Bearshide
CURLEWIS William E.	—	—
CURTIS William John	Fairlight	—
DAVID Lewis	Martello No. 62	Cuckmere Haven
DOUGLAS John	—	No. 1 Battery Sandown
DREW George	—	No. 2 Battery Sandown
DUFFELL John	—	Fort Moncrieff
EARLE E. G.	Camber	Camber
EVANS John	Seasalter	Seasalter
EVERSFIELD Thomas	—	Ecclesbourne
FERRAR William Augustus	Crowlink	Crowlink
FOSTER Henry D.	—	Copperas Gap
FRANKLIN Edward	Hove	Hove
GAHAN George	Martello No. 4	Martello No. 4

*Not listed as such, probably Martello No. 46.

HILIS John	Goring	Elmer
HIRE Frederick	Haddicks (sic)	Haddicks
HOWES George	Bognor	Bognor
HUMPHREYS George	—	Milton (Feversham)
HUNTER Robert	—	Seasalter
HUNTER Valentine	—	Conyers (Feversham)
JOACHIM R.	Greenway	Greenway
JOHNSTON Charles A.	—	Westbrook
JONES H. B.	Thorney	Wallend
KELLY Richard Nugent	Ramsgate	Kingsferry
KORTRIGHT Alfred	Felpham	Cockbush
LASTON Samuel H.	—	—
LAWLESS Henry	—	Pegwell Bay
LETWORTHY Henry	West Wittering	Worthing
LONGLEY James M.	—	Newgate
LOVELESS James	—	—
McTAVISH Archibald	Rye	*Adder*
MARSHALL William	—	North End (Deal)
MORGAN Richard	Jury's Gap	Camber
MOTTLEY John M.	Martello No. 50	Martello No. 50
MURRAY John E. F.	Sandwich (Shingle End)	Seasalter Cliff
NAGLE Archibald	Shellness	—
NICKOLLS James Harvey	Rye	*Enchantress*
PALMER George	Martello No. 48	Priory
PENNINGTON Thomas	Rye	Martello No. 38
PITFIELD Jacob	—	—
POOLE Robert	Sheerness	—
POYNTER C. W.	Deal	*Pelter* Brig
PRATT James	Black Rock	Black Rock
PRATTENT John	Holywell	Holywell
PUCKETT Charles	—	Beresford (Feversham)
PYM Richard	—	—
RAWSTORNE James	Cuckmere Haven	Cuckmere Haven
RAYMOND James G.	Hastings	Hastings
REAY Joseph	—	—
RIDDLE John	—	Elmley Ferry
ROSE Thomas	Fort Twiss	Fort Twiss
SERVANTE Charles	Martello No. 42	Martello No. 42
SHORT Henry M.	Newhaven	—
STONE	Bexhill	Galley Hill
STUART James	—	Fort Moncrieff
TURNER Charles	— .	Bishopstone
WESTBROOK George F.	—	—
WESTBROOK Edmond B.	—	—
WHEELER Thomas P.	—	Swalecliff
WHITE George Robert	—	—
WIGHT Alexander (?)	Martello No. 23	Martello No. 23
WILLIAMS John	Newhaven	—
WILLIAMS Thomas M.	Brighton	Brighton
WINNETT (?) William	Wallend	Littlehampton
WISE Chapman	—	Swale Cliff
WOODHAM William H.	Stokes Bay (?)	Stokes Bay
WRIGHT G. M. M.	Newhaven	Newhaven

Author's Special Note

Mrs Eileen Weston's contribution to this book must not pass unacknowledged, for it was by her diligent application that the foregoing list and also that of the Blockade Stations were collated from various diffuse and dusty sources in Admiralty records (see p.135). She is now embarked upon a task which we lesser mortals would find even more daunting—that of listing, and then indexing, the entire set of the Muster Books of *Severn, Hyperion, Ramillies* and *Talavera*. With the completion of this project, the names and various other details of well over 2,000 ratings of the Coast Blockade will have been preserved for posterity in an accessible form. Anyone interested in further details of this scheme is invited to write to Mrs Weston, 16 Pitfold Road, Lee SE12 9HX, enclosing a stamped addressed envelope.

It will also be of interest to note that an Index of Coastguards, containing thousands of references, has already been formed; it is certain that many ex-Blockaders appear therein. Full details may be obtained from Mrs E. R. Stage, 150 Fulwell Park Avenue, Twickenham TW2 5HB, enclosing a stamped addressed envelope.

Prison-ship in Portsmouth Harbour.   (E. W. Cooke, 1825)
George Ransley was confined here for 3 months prior to transportation. (see page 114)

Appendix B—
The Ships and the Stations

Bathurst 10

A brig, purchased at Port Jackson in 1821 and used to survey the Australian coast until 1824 when posted to the Blockade and stationed at West Swale. Transferred to Coast Guard 1833, last mentioned 1862.

Enchantress 14

A sloop, 80′ long, carrying fourteen 6 pounders. Built Sutton's Yard 1802, purchased 1804. Posted to Harbour Service 1813, in 1826 she was ballasted and beached at Old Rye Harbour to accommodate personnel of the Western Division of the Coast Blockade. Broken up 1869.

Ganymede 26

Originally the French frigate *Hebe*, captured and renamed 1809. A 6th-rater, 127′ long armed with twenty-two 32 pounders, four 6 pounders and ten 18 pounder carronades. The original Blockade HQ ship, she was posted to Woolwich in 1822 to become a convict hulk. There she eventually capsized and was broken up in 1838.

Highflyer 2

Tender to *Hyperion*, 56′ long and mounting two 6 pounders. Built at Woolwich dockyard, sold 1833 to Ledger of Rotherhithe.

Hyperion 40

Built by Gibson of Hull in 1807, a 5th-rater frigate, 144′ long carrying twenty-eight 18 pounders and twelve 6 pounders. The Newhaven Blockade HQ ship 1825-31, she was broken up at Portsmouth in 1833.

Industry

Built by Warwick-Eling 1804, a transport vessel some 100′ long and carrying four 12 pounder carronades. Posted to Harbour Service in 1820, she served the Blockade as tender to *Ramillies* and later to *Talavera*. Broken up 1846.

Ramillies 74

Built 1785 by Randall of Rotherhithe, 170′ long, armed with twenty-eight 32 pounders, twenty-eight 18 pounders and eighteen 9 pounders, she fought at Ushant ('the Glorious First of June') in 1794 against the French, was present with Nelson at Copenhagen in 1801 and took part in action against the Americans at New Orleans in 1814. She then passed to Harbour Service and was the main Blockade HQ ship, anchored off Deal, 1823-31. With the Blockade's disbandment, she was stationed as a quarantine vessel in the Medway and was broken up at Deptford in 1850.

Severn 50

A 4th-rate frigate mounting twenty 32 pounders, twenty-eight 24 pounders and two 9 pounders. Built by Wigram and Green of Blackwall in 1813, she was 159′ long and experimentally constructed of pitch pine instead of the usual oak which was then in short supply. About fifty frigates and sloops were built of this material, all were useless after a few years. She did however, see her share of action, being engaged in mid-Atlantic (January 1814) by a superior French force (*Sultane* and *Etoile*) from whom she escaped. She served on the American seaboard in 1814 and was present at the Algiers action in August 1816. She was sold to Ledger of Rotherhithe in 1825 after some six years Blockade service off Deal.

Talavera 74

A similar vessel to *Ramillies*, built at Woolwich in 1816, launched as *Thunderer* and renamed the following year. Her main claim to fame appears to be that she transported a sphinx from Egypt to England in 1839. She was accidentally destroyed by fire at Plymouth in the following year.

A Coastal Blockade Station at Rye Old Harbour—the sloop Enchantress. (Old print)

Wolf 8

Built by White of Cowes in 1826. A cutter 55′ long, armed with six 6 pounders and two 3 pounders her first duty was with the Custom Service, passing to the Blockade as tender to *Hyperion*. Broken up at Portsmouth 1829.

N.B. 'Posted to Harbour Service' denotes that the ship had been adjudged unfit for service on the open sea in action but was not decrepit enough to warrant breaking up.

The Coast Blockade Stations

(Compiled from the original Admiralty records ca. 1830)

Many of these stations were taken over by the Coast Guard when the Blockade disbanded. The map (back end-paper) shows the Coast Guard stations at about 1850; even then many of the old Blockade stations are still identifiable. Sheila Sutcliffe's *Martello Towers* (David and Charles 1972) contains much interesting incidental information.

The stations are listed in order beginning in the Thames estuary and proceed round the coast almost to the Isle of Wight.

Sheerness	Epple Bay
Queensborough	Westbrook
Bathurst	Newgate
Elmsley Ferry (*Snapper*)	Kingsgate
Scrap's Gate	Broadstairs
East End Lane	Ramsgate
Hensbrook	Pegwell
Warden Point	North Shore
Leysdown	Shingle End
Shellness	No. 1 Battery Sandown
Harty	No. 2 Battery Sandown
Pioneer	Sandown Castle
Beresford	Deal
Graveney	Walmer
Seasalter	Kingsdown
Whitstable	Old Stairs
Tankerton	St Margarets
Swale Cliff	Cornhill
Herne Bay	Casemates (Dover)
Bishopston	Townsend Battery (Dover)
Reculvers	Lydden Spout
St Nicholas	Hougham (replaced by *Pelter* brig)

Martello No. 1†
Martello No. 3†
Folkestone
Martello No. 4†
Shorne Cliff (sic)
Fort Twiss (Hythe)
Fort Sutherland (Hythe)
Fort Moncrieff (Hythe)
Martello No. 22 (Dymchurch)
Martello No. 23† (Dymchurch)
Martello No. 24† (Dymchurch)*
Martello No. 26 (St Mary's Bay)
Martello No. 27 (St Mary's Bay)
Littlestone
Romney ·
No. 1 Battery Dungeness
No. 2 Battery Dungeness
Grand Redoubt
Lydd
Jury's Gap
Camber Watch-house
Guard-boat *Congo*
   (later replaced by *Adder* then *Dwarf)*
Enchantress (beached in Rye Harbour)
Martello No. 30†
Winchelsea
Martello No. 31 (Pett Level)
Martello No. 33 (Pett Level)
Martello No. 36 (Pett Level)
Martello No. 38 (Pett Level)
Haddocks
Fairlight
Ecclesbourne
Town Watch-house (Hastings)
Priory
Martello No. 39 (St Leonards)
Martello No. 40 ('hospital')
Martello No. 41
   (Bulverhythe, demolished by 1842)
Martello No. 42
   (Bulverhythe, demolished by 1842)
Martello No. 44 (Galley Hill)
Martello No. 46
Martello No. 48
Martello No. 49
Martello No. 50 (Cooden Beach)
Martello No. 51 (Cooden Beach)
Martello No. 53 (Cooden Beach)

Martello No. 55† (Norman's Bay)
Martello No. 57 (Pevensey Bay)
Martello No. 59 (Pevensey Bay)
Martello No. 62† (Pevensey Bay)
Martello No. 64† (Pevensey Bay)
East Langley (Langney) Fort
Martello No. 71 (Langney Point)
Martello No. 72 (Langney Point)
Eastbourne ('hospital')
Martello No. 73† (Eastbourne)**
Holywell
Beachyhead (sic)
Birling Gap
Crowlink
Cuckmere Haven
Martello No. 74† (Seaford)
Blatchington
Newhaven
Bearshide
Salt Dean (sic)
Greenway
Blackrock
Brighton
Hove
Copperas Gap (Fishersgate)
Shoreham
Lancing
East Worthing
West Worthing
Kingston
Goring
Littlehampton
East Elmer
West Elmer
Felpham
Bognor
Pagham
Wallend
Selsey Bill
Thorney
Cockbush
Chichester Harbour (watch-vessel)

† Still standing.
* Restored and open to the public.
** Now a public monument, the Wish Tower as it is now called houses an interesting collection of local items.

Appendix C—Some
Naval Terminology

Boatswain

The oldest rank in the Royal Navy, usually abbreviated to Bosun. One of the 'Standing Officers' (see p.45), this Warrant Officer saw to the running and the working of the ship —

'the hated man with the rattan cane and pipes whose combined efforts made the poor seamen jump to it every hour of the day and if necessary of the night'.

Brig

More accurately, the brig-sloop derived from the brigantine. It was a two-masted square-rigged vessel, the all-purpose small ship. Carried up to sixteen 32-pdr carronades, with two 'long 6s' as chase guns — a formidable force capable of sailing anywhere in the world as long as supplies could be maintained.

Cannon

The 'big guns' were identified and described by the weight of the ball they threw e.g. 3-, 6-, 12-, 18-, 24-, 32-pounders and so on. Each type came in two versions, the 'long' which was more accurate and the 'short' the more devastating especially at short range (up to 300 yards). A 'long 32' measured 9′ 6″ weighed 3 tons and took a charge of 11lbs of powder. Its effective range was more than one mile.

Carronade

First cast in 1779 in the Scottish town of Carron, hence the name. A short, squat piece, lighter than the equivalent cannon (although some took 68-pound balls), it was known as the 'smasher' or 'devil gun' from its devastating close range effect. It had several drawbacks, the most dangerous being its

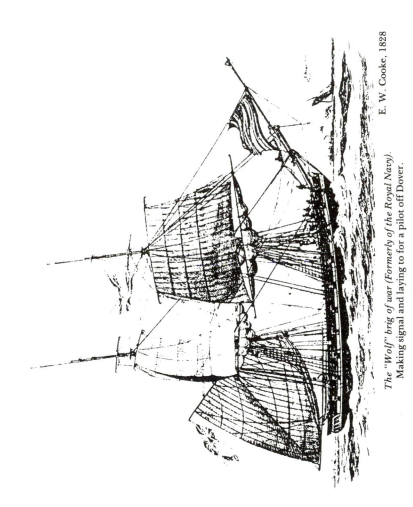

E. W. Cooke, 1828

The "Wolf" brig of war (Formerly of the Royal Navy).
Making signal and laying to for a pilot off Dover.

violent recoil which tended to split its carriage and dismount it thus not only killing the men who served it but also putting itself out of action.

Cruiser/Cruizer

Any vessel detached from the main fleet for independent duties e.g. reconnaissance or anti-smuggling patrol. Speed was vital, a frigate was often employed.

Cutter

A small vessel, 'fore-and-aft rigged' (i.e. with sails like a yacht) common in the English Channel. With its single mast, it was similar to a sloop except that the straight bowsprit could be run in on deck if needed.

Cutting-out

This was the manoeuvre employed to get between any enemy vessel and the shore and capturing it. It was usually carried out by small boats rowed out from the parent ship.

Frigate

Relatively small, very fast and highly manoeuvrable, this warship was 'ship-rigged' (i.e. with sails carried on cross-pieces or 'yards') and had a single gun-deck. Did not fight in the 'line of battle' (see Ships' Ratings below) but was employed upon reconnaissance, message carrying and anti-smuggling duties.

Half-pay

If no employment could be found for an otherwise eligible officer, he was 'put on half-pay'; there were no pension schemes as such for officers although, if in very dire straits and disabled they were eligible for admission to the Royal Naval Hospital at Greenwich.

Landsman/Landman

'A very low form of marine life, carrying a minimum of wages', this rating was introduced in the 1790s and was usually applied to the newly-joined man who had never been to sea before and had no craft qualification.

Lieutenant's Appointment

The required minimum length of service was six years, of which two had to be as Midshipman and two as Master's Mate. The candidate was duly interviewed by a Board of Admirals; certificates of sobriety, diligence and ability, along with a Journal, were required to be produced and an examination conducted

'to ascertain that he could efficiently splice, knot, reef a sail, work a ship in sailing, shift his tides, keep a reckoning of the ship's way by plain sailing and Mercator, observe by sun and stars and find the variations of a compass, and is qualified to do the duty of an Able Seaman and a Midshipman'.

Success at the interview signified eligibility for a commission but did not guarantee its immediate grant; this depended upon the availability of a suitable ship.

Master's Mate

An obsolete rank, roughly equivalent to Sub-Lieutenant. His duties were to assist the Master (see p.44) in all matters concerned with navigating the ship.

Midshipman

The first step up from Volunteer to Sea Officer although in the latter half of the 18th century middle-aged Midshipmen from the Lower Deck were not uncommon.

Post-Captain

The 'captain' of an unrated ship (see Ships' Ratings) was a Lieutenant, in a frigate he was a Commander, but a ship of the line warranted a full Captain in command; hence the term Post-Captain to denote that the actual rank had been reached. From then on, promotion to Flag rank was slow but sure (see p.43).

Privateer

A merchant ship furnished with an authority from its government (a 'Letter of Marque') permitting its Captain to wage war on enemy shipping. The crew wore no uniform, nor was the ship compelled to fly her colours during an engagement. The 'Letter' cost the owners £3,000 if the crew totalled 150 or more, £1,500 if less; a share was allowed on the sale of captured vessels and their cargo. The system, centuries old, was not universally abolished until 1898.

Quartermaster

In general, an old, tried and trusted senior petty officer responsible for the correct stowage and care of provisions, the correct coiling of the ship's cables in their tiers and the punctual sounding of the ship's bell. In the Coast Blockade service, however, many were young active men fully engaged in leading their men against the smugglers; QM (1st Class) Richard Morgan (see p.111) was one of these.

Ships' Ratings

The larger vessels of the Royal Navy were classified or rated according to the number of guns carried. Largest of all were the 'first-raters', 2,500 ton monsters, eight times the length of a cricket pitch, carrying 100-120 guns and up to a thousand men; at the bottom of the league came the sixth-rate frigates (600 tons, 180 crew) a mere six cricket pitches long. In Nelson's day, the 'line of battle' (hence 'ship of the line') was formed by the 1st, 2nd and 3rd-raters; they were the only craft stout enough to withstand the full force of a French broadside; the lower 'rates' were used for reconnaissance and patrol — they played the major role in our blockade of the French Channel ports.

There were of course even smaller vessels — ship-sloops, cutters, bomb-ketches, gun-brigs, rocket-boats and the like — which were unrated, but the number of guns they carried was often stated after the ship's name e.g. *Highflyer* 2. It should be realised that this figure indicates only the number of regulation pattern cannon; it did not include the carronades and it was therefore quite possible for a light vessel carrying carronades to pack a far heavier short-range punch than another which, by the figure after her name, appeared to

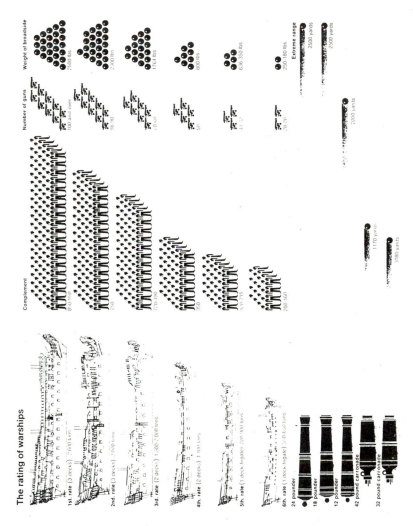

Reproduced by kind permission *Newnes Books*.

have the heavier armament. One reason for this apparent anomaly was said to be financial; a small vessel crammed with carronades would have as high a short-range fire power as a 'rated' ship, but she would still be commanded by a junior officer whose pay was much below that of the Post-Captain required to command a ship of the line or that of a Commander in a lower rated vessel.

Sloop

Similar to a Cutter but having a fixed bowsprit and smaller sails. Note, however, that the ship-sloop and the brig-sloop which were brought out at the end of the Napoleonic wars were ship-rigged (see Frigate).

Volunteer

They were of two classes, Man and Boy. The Men were often classified as Landsmen Volunteers; the Voluntary aspect was sometimes doubtful as quite often they had been sent along by the magistrate as an alternative to a prison sentence.

The Boys were further subdivided:

Boy 1st Class:

'To consist of Young Gentlemen intended for the Sea Service . . . to be styled Volunteers and paid £6 per annum'.

These were the future Sea Officers (see p.43). There was no minimum age requirement; Captains were limited in the number they were allowed to take—but there were ways around this regulation (see Biographical Note on Thomas Hamilton p.121).

Boy 2nd Class:

'To consist of Boys between 15 and 17 years of age, to be divided into watches with the seamen in order to make them such, at £5 per annum'.

From these were drawn the future Petty and Warrant Officers.

Boy 3rd Class:

'To consist of Boys between the age of 13 and 15 years of age, to be attendants upon Officers, at £4 per annum'.

This rating replaced the old one of 'Officer's Servant' in 1794.

The usual portal of entry for a Young Gentleman was by a 'Captain's Letter'.

(see page 143)

Appendix D

Captain William McCulloch RN (1782-1825)
Record of Service

Dates	Rank	Ship	Rating & guns	Captain(s)	Station(s)	Remarks
21. 4.98- 6. 6.03	Midshipman	*Diomede*	4/50	Hon Chas Elphinstone Samuel Mottley Wm Fothergill	East Indies/ C. of Good Hope	
7. 6.03- 5. 4.05	Midshipman	*Egyptienne*	5/40	Thos Larcom Hon Chas Fleming	Channel/ St Helena/ Ferrol/ W. Isles	
6. 4.05- —. 8.05	Midshipman	*Northumberland*	3/74	Geo Cochrane	Leeward Islands	Flag-ship of Rear-Adml. Hon. Alex Cochrane
—. 8.05- 18.12.05	Lieutenant	*Alligator*	6/28	F.A.Collier	Leeward Islands	
19.12.05- 1. 4.06	Lieutenant	*Princess Charlotte*	5/38	Geo Tobin	Leeward Islands	
2. 4.06- 22. 1.07	Lieutenant	*Galatea*	5/32	Geo Sayer	Leeward Islands	
23. 1.07- 8.6.07	Lieutenant	*Melville*	Brig-Sloop 18	Isaac Ferrieres Hon. Jas W. King	Leeward Islands	
9. 6.07- 6.12.07	Lieutenant	*Dart*	Lugger/8	E. Rushworth D. Brainer	Leeward Island	*Dart* was originally French, then a British privateer
7.12.07- 28.11.08	Lieutenant	*Latona*	5/38	Jas A. Wood	Leeward Islands	
29.11.08- 7. 1.09	Lieutenant	*Neptune*	2/98	Chas Dilkes	Leeward Islands	Flag-ship of Rear-Adml Sir Alex Cochrane
8. 1.09- 31. 7.09	Flag Lieutenant	*Neptune*	2/98	Chas Dilkes	Leeward Islands	Flag-ship of Rear-Adml Sir Alex Cochrane
1. 8.09- 21. 1.10	Flag Lieutenant	*Pompee*	3/80	Chas Dilkes	Leeward Islands	Flag-ship of Vice-Adml Sir Alex Cochrane
22. 1.10 30. 6.10	Commander	*Asp*	Sloop/16		Leeward Islands	
1. 7.10- 15. 7.11	Commander	*St Christopher*	Sloop/18		Leeward Islands	Ex French privateer
16.11.12- 16. 4.14	Commander	*Heron*	Sloop/16		Leeward Islands	
17. 4.14- 1. 7.14	Post Captain	*Venerable*	3/74		Leeward Islands	
2. 7.14- 8.1.15	Post Captain	*Barrossa*	5/36		Leeward Islands	Flag-ship of Rear-Adml P. C. Durh
11. 7.15- 25. 8.15	Post Captain	*Ganymede*	6/26		Portsmouth	
26. 8.15- 23. 5.17	Post Captain	*Ganymede*	6/26		Downs	Coast Blockade
24. 5.17- —.—.23	Post Captain	*Severn*	4/50		Downs	Coast Blockade
—.—.23- 25.10.25	Post Captain	*Ramillies*	3/74		Downs	Coast Blockade Died 25.10.25

Appendix E

The Family Background of Captain William McCulloch RN

Just north of Gatehouse is Cardoness Castle, a ruined 15th century tower-house of four storeys above a vaulted basement with originally stairway, stone benches and elaborate fireplaces. The tower belonged originally to the de Cardines but, after 1450, to the McCullochs. The road skirts Cairnharrow (1,496′) and runs above wooded and rocky Ravenshall Point, just west of which it crosses Kirkdale Burn. On the shore, 250 yards east of the burn's mouth, is the narrow entrance to Dirk Hatteraich's Cave*, the largest of several here. Near the entrance to the glen, in the woods, are the remains of Barholm Castle, a 16th-17th century McCulloch stronghold. (*Blue Guide to Scotland,* J. Tomes 1972.)

Family Tree

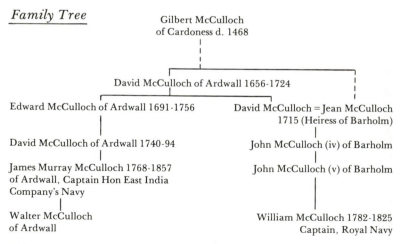

Gilbert McCulloch
of Cardoness d. 1468

David McCulloch of Ardwall 1656-1724

Edward McCulloch of Ardwall 1691-1756

David McCulloch of Ardwall 1740-94

James Murray McCulloch 1768-1857
of Ardwall, Captain Hon East India
Company's Navy

Walter McCulloch
of Ardwall

David McCulloch = Jean McCulloch
1715 (Heiress of Barholm)

John McCulloch (iv) of Barholm

John McCulloch (v) of Barholm

William McCulloch 1782-1825
Captain, Royal Navy

*Dirk Hatteraich was the smuggler in Scott's *Guy Mannering*.

146

Cardoness Castle, ancient stronghold of the McCullochs of Galloway.

Capt. McCulloch's memorial tablet St. Leonard's Churchyard, Deal.

The Arms of McCulloch of Barholm.

Both branches of the family originate from Gilbert McCulloch who died *ca* 1468. For the ensuing 250 years, the two limbs of the family tree lived at a distance of some ten miles until the heiress of Barholm married a younger son of the Ardwall branch in 1715, thus re-uniting the lines. William McCulloch was the son of John McCulloch (v)'s second wife, Jessie MacFarlane. The house at Barholm was a small Georgian property, delightfully situated, built *ca* 1747. It was

148

demolished some twenty years ago; a bungalow stands on the site.

On the 20th September 1810, not long after promotion to independent command, William McCulloch married 19-year-old Jane Osborne in Antigua. In the register of St Leonard's, Deal, and St Mary's, Walmer are recorded the baptisms of their eight children from between 1816 and 1825. (Their first, Anna, was actually born at Barholm in 1812 but was not christened until 1816.)

After McCulloch's death, his widow left the Port Admiral's Residence in Deal and moved to Harbledown, Canterbury. Granted an Admiralty pension, she lived on until 1853; the line of McCulloch of Barholm is now extinct.

Hasting's smugglers at work loading goods at Bo-Peep.
(Drawing by Paul Hardy)

Appendix F—

An Extract from a Report made to The Treasury by the Customs Commissioners

THE TWELFTH REPORT of the COMMISSIONERS appointed by His Royal Highness The Prince Regent, to inquire into the existing Regulations for the conduct of Business, in every department of the CUSTOMS . . . with a view to suggest such alterations therein, as may be considered necessary for facilitating the dispatch of Business, for affording accommodation to Trade, and for securing and improving the Revenue.

. . . It remains for us now to speak of the peculiar force which is established upon one part of the coast; viz: between the Isle of Sheppey and Beachy Head, for the prevention of smuggling, and which is applicable to the district exclusively, without having any connexion with the general system; we mean the coast blockade, an account of the origin and present state of which is inserted in the Appendix.

We have made the best enquiries within our power concerning the efficiency of this establishment, and its success in preventing the landing of contraband goods. We are upon the whole convinced that the revenue has derived a very considerable protection from it; and that by the vigilance, activity and resolution of Captain McCulloch, and the officers serving under him, the smugglers have been greatly baffled, in a district peculiarly adapted to their practices, and where they have been accustomed to receive so much encouragement and assistance from the inveterate habits of a great part of the population. We are aware, however, that even this rigorous blockade is not so completely effectual as entirely to prevent smuggling on that part of the coast; we have undoubted information of contraband cargoes having been successfully landed within its limits and we have no reason to suppose that the same thing may have occurred in many other instances . . . we have contemplated the very great number of desertions from this force (and are led to believe that) a great part of them must have been occasioned by corrupt collusion between the blockade men and the smugglers. We are also bound to state, that we have no ground for concluding, that this naval blockade has been more successful than the preventive water guard might have been, if applied to the same coast . . . yet we cannot feel warranted in recommending to your Lordships the removal of this naval blockade at the present time . . . The inconvenience, and even the danger of any alteration under present circumstances are sufficiently obvious. We shall, therefore, confine ourselves to urging the general advantage of a combined system, without presuming to direct your Lordships' judgement, as to the time or mode of obtaining that advantage by the reduction of this blockade, and the substitution of a strengthened preventive system upon the line which it now occupies; observing only, that the difference between the expense of the preventive guard and of the coast blockade, is so considerable as to admit of establishing the former upon a highly increased scale of strength . . . and of still making a considerable saving, as compared with the annual charge of the coast blockade . . . *(the Report then recommends stationing soldiers and marines in the south-east to assist either the Coast Blockade or the Preventive Waterguard whenever threatened by overwhelming presence of smugglers)* . . . every principle of policy, and every consideration of humanity forbid, that the means employed against these deluded persons should be either really, or apparently, so nearly balanced within their own strength, as to give any degree of encouragement to men stimulated as they are, by the prospect of great gain, to undertake, or to protract so pernicious a contest.

(signed) CHARLES LONG
GRANVILLE C. H. SOMERSET
R. FREWIN
J. C. HERRIES
W. J. LUSHINGTON

Office of Inquiry into the
Customs &c. 31st July 1821

Appendix No 6 to the Report

Coast Blockade

In the year 1816, Captain McCulloch, of His Majesty's ship *Ganymede* (which was one of the vessels employed in the prevention of smuggling, between Dungeness and the North Foreland), suggested the plan of landing the crews of the vessels employed on this service, a little after sunset, for the purpose of forming a guard along the coast during the night, such crews to return to their ships in the morning, a few minutes before sunrise.

The success of this experiment, led to the adoption of that method of guarding the coast upon a more extended and permanent principle.

After a survey made by Rear Admiral Rowley, and upon a report from that officer, relating to the details of the proposed arrangement, the Lords of the Treasury gave their final directions for carrying it into effect, by a minute dated the 19th June 1817.

Under this authority, the district included between the North and South Forelands, was assigned to Captain McCulloch, with the officers and crew of His Majesty's ship *Severn,* acting under the orders of the Lords of the Admiralty. The boats and men, belonging to the preventive service, which had previously been stationed between those points were withdrawn, and the protection of that part of the coast was then left exclusively to this force, now called the naval blockade.

This blockade was afterwards extended on the one side, from the North Foreland to the Isle of Sheppey, and on the other, from the South Foreland to Beachy Head. This extent of the coast is now formed into *three divisions*, each of those divisions being again sub-divided into *four districts*.

The divisions are each under the superintendence of a senior lieutenant, a midshipman, one petty officer of the first class, and one of the second class. The districts are each under the superintendence of a junior lieutenant.

The men are divided into parties of ten each, who have to guard about a mile of coast, five being on duty at a time; and guard-houses are stationed along the coast, about the distance of four miles from each other.

The seamen volunteer into the service; and if found effective, of good character, and not locally connected, they are accepted.

They engage to serve for three years.

The pay is the same as if borne on the books of any of His Majesty's ships. The number of persons employed in the year ending 5th January 1820 and 5th January 1821, respectively were.

In the year ending 5th January 1820 - - - 1,253
In the year ending 5th January 1821 - - - 1,276

The expenses of this establishment were.

For the year ending 5th January 1820 - - - £85,428.8.4½
For the year ending 5th January 1821 - - - £89,152.8.4½

Appendix G—
The Blockade in Fiction

Although stories about smugglers and revenue men are legion, it is very seldom that contemporary writers ever mention the Coast Blockade as such. Captain W. N. Glascock RN however, in his *A Naval Sketchbook* (First Series) in 1831 relates the following in his chapter headed *Coast Blockade*:
(NB the punctuation is as the original version).

A Tale

It was late in the afternoon of a gloomy day in the latter part of November, when, in consequence of a signal made that a suspicious sail was seen off the coast, as if waiting for the flowing of the tide in the dark, Lieutenant . . . had given orders to man his favourite galley, and proceed in quest of the stranger. The crew had been carefully, though to appearance hastily, selected from those inured to service, and bearing a character for intrepidity, some of whom had been the partners of an enterprize which was ever uppermost in his mind, when, amongst the first to board the American frigate *Chesapeake*, as a young midshipman, he was stretched on the deck by the stroke of a cutlass on the head. The strokesman of the boat, whose brawny arms had borne him that memorable day to the cockpit of the *Shannon*, as soon as the Americans had deserted their deck, and fled for safety below, as he now shipped the rudder, looked wistfully in the wind's eye. The glance was not unobserved; but the lieutenant, apprehensive that it might be accompanied by some remonstrance (a liberty which *Jack* considered himself exclusively privileged to take), quietly motioned him to go forward, in order to hoist the main-sail. The boat being shoved off the beach, after pitching twice in the surf, rose triumphantly over the third sea, which had now exhausted itself. In a moment the sail was hoisted; she instantly gathered way, and stood-off in a lateral direction from the shore. The men seated themselves regularly on the thwarts, and the strokesman, after receiving the main-sheet through the fair-leader abaft, sat with it in his hand in such a position on the after-thwart, that, though his face was turned to wind-ward, his eye would occasionally meet that of his commander. As the light-boat lay down to the wind, and became steady in her course towards the chase, the crew had time to look around them. The strokesman's eye was alternately turned from that part of the heavens, where he had vainly sought for any encouraging appearances amidst the portentious indications of a wild wintry sky, to the beach; where, in a lonely romantic gorge, skirted with verdure and leafless underwood, between two grey beetling cliffs, was discovered the compact white-wooden station house of the party, with its signal-post and miniature glacis descending almost to high-watermark. His look betrayed unusual emotion, in one of his years and service, possibly occasioned by the intrusive officiousness of the remembrance, that there were garnered up the source of his best affections—his wife and innocent little prattlers, whom, through some unaccountable presentiment, he foreboded he should never see more. A tear might have glazed the veteran's eye at the moment; for, as if unwilling to be longer a witness of the struggle between tenderness and duty, the lieutenant addressed him in a tone of evidently assumed ease, and enquired if the armschest had been kept dry? Receiving an answer in the affirmative, and having ascertained that each man had his cutlass beside him, he proceeded to examine the priming of his pistols, which he finally placed in his waistbelt, and wrapped himself in a cloak which had been spread for him in the stern-sheets abaft. Taking advantage of the first heavy swell, he rose in the boat to catch a glimpse of the strange sail in the offing, which discovered broad on the lee-bow. Having directed the attention of the bow-man to her position, both resumed their seats, and the lieutenant shaped his course to board her on the quarter. Not a word, as yet, had escaped the lips of any of his men, who sat cowering in a bending attitude, with elevated shoulders and arms crossed, fearful of changing the position of a limb, lest it should occasion any alteration in the boat's trim. Thus aided by every effort of art, and impelled by a light breeze, the galley soon gained rapidly on the chase; which, perceiving that the boat from the shore was evidently about to pursue her, bore round-up, making all the sail she could carry before the wind. The bow-man, just then looking under the foot of the lug, pronounced her to be a large lugger, which he had before seen on the station, under similarly suspicious circumstances. The lieutenant, putting up the helm, instantly edged into her wake, and followed precisely her track. A short period, however, sufficed to show that the chase, from the quantity of sail she was enabled to carry, had decidedly the advantage; and the wind continuing to freshen as the tide set in, she rapidly distanced her pursuer. In half-an-hour she was hull down; the haze of evening growing every moment thicker, she became almost imperceptible to the view. The men now involuntarily turned their eyes, which had hitherto been strained on the chase, to the stern of the galley; the appeal was unnecessary — the lieutenant was already occupied in council with the coxswain; his trusty favourite hesitated not to dissuade him, in terms respectful, yet decisive, from continuing so unequal a chase; more particularly as there was no chance, in the dark, of communicating by signal, either with the shore or with any cruizer which might be then off the station. A heavy swell now set in from the same point in which the wind had continued all day. The sun had set with every indication of stormy weather; a pale yellow streak of light over the land, partly reflected on the east, formed the only contrast to the general murky gloom of the horizon; across which the gull, and other sea-fowl, hastily fled the approach of the gale, already indicated by the swift drifting of the scud, which overtook them in their flight, and suddenly enveloped all in darkness, without the intervention of twilight. They had got so far to leeward, that to return with the lug was impossible. The sail had already been lowered, the mast struck, and the boat brought head to wind; when the crew, shipping their oars, bent their broad shoulders to pull her through the heavy sea, which flung itself in sheets of spray over the bows, and drenched every man on board. It was soon found that oars were unavailing to contend against the force of a sea like this, in which it was scarcely possible so small and delicate a bark should live much longer. The waves were rolling from the main with aggravated violence, and the united strength of the men could barely keep her head to wind; who, perceiving there was no longer the slightest prospect of making any progress, or the wind moderating, sullenly contented themselves with hanging on their oars. Apprehension soon put an end to all insubordination. Remonstrances on the impossibility of successfully persevering in their present course, were now muttered by every seaman, except the coxswain, whose features betrayed, notwithstanding, no less anxiety than the rest. A heavy sea, which now struck the starboard bow, making, in consequence of its being impossible for the crew to keep the boat's head on, a rapid accumulation of water every minute, soon decided the reluctant lieutenant to run (though at the obvious hazard of her destruction) the boat ashore in the first situation which might offer a chance of saving the lives of his brave companions. 'Lay in your oars, my lads,' cried he; 'step the short mast—close-reef the storm-lug: we must run all hazards, and beach the galley under canvas.' Whilst executing this order, the bow-man sung out, 'a sail close aboard, sir; if she don't keep her luff, she'll run us right down.'—'Luff, luff!' exclaimed aloud every man in the boat. The lugger's course, however, remaining unaltered, there could now be no doubt that she had seen them first, and perceiving her to be a king's boat, her object was to run clean over the galley, by taking her right abeam. Destruction appeared inevitable in their helpless condition. A shriek of despair, mingled with execrations, succeeded as she neared the galley, when the lieutenant rose in the boat, levelled his pistol at the steersman, and fired: the hand which grasped the tiller relaxed its hold, and the miscreant his life. The lugger instantly broached-to, passing to the windward of the boat, — 'Out oars, my lads,' said the lieutenant, 'we'll board the villains.' Aye, aye sir,' exclaimed several voices, with an alacrity which might be taken for the surest earnest of meditated revenge. The oars were again manned, the boat in the meantime pitching bows under, and shipping green seas fore-and-aft. Before she had got way on her, two of the weather oars snapt short in the rowelocks, and her intention to board being suspected by the smuggler, she had no sooner paid-off, so as to get the wind again abaft the beam, than shaping a course edging in for the land, she quickly dropped the galley astern. Having run so far to leeward in the former chase, no one was now able to decide on what part of the shore an attempt to land might be practicable: all was darkness around; and although, from two or three flashes, discernible at an elevation considerably above the sea, and which appeared to be signals made from the heights to assist the desperate outlaws they had just encountered, there was no doubt they could be at no great distance from the land, still to follow her was to brave unseen dangers. The men were clamorous to hoist the lug and give chase; a sentiment in which the unpresuming coxswain concurred, as he observed, 'that capture or no capture, they were more likely to find a smooth by following the lugger, which clearly was herself making for the beach.' A heavy lurch, which nearly swamped the boat, soon created unanimity. The lug was hoisted at all hazards and the lieutenant putting the helm up, she flew with inconceivable velocity in the lugger's wake, though not without imminent danger of being pooped by every successive sea. The roaring of the surf was now distinctly heard: and soon the whole scene was lighted-up by its luminous appearance.

The bow-man, alarmed, now vociferated, 'Breakers a-head!—hard-down, sir, hard-down!' Before the word was repeated she had entered the frightfully agitated element—'Down with the sail, or we're lost!' exclaimed the crew—'Hold-on! hold-on every thing!' cried the veteran, ''tis our only chance to beach her.' The surf now reared itself in boiling masses higher than the mast, and as it fell, thundering on the shore, the wild din burst on the affrighted ears of the seamen like successive salvoes of heavy artillery. An enormous sea, striking her on the quarter, swept her broadside to the surf, washing out the lieutenant, with one of the crew: and the next, bursting with wilder fury, turned her bottom-upwards, burying beneath her the seven unhappy seamen in one common grave.

The Coast Blockade Station, Pegwell Bay, Ramsgate, 1819.
(An original drawing, from the Lapthorne Collection)
'There were garnered up the source of his bert affections . . .' (see page 155)

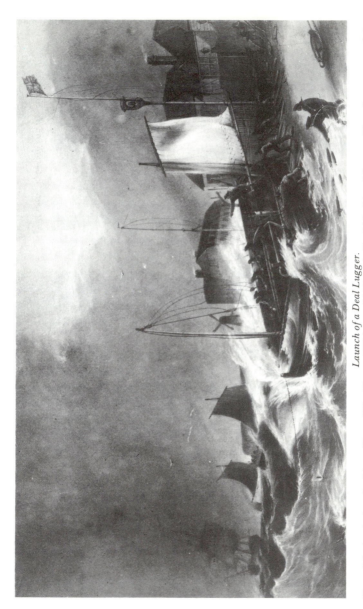

Launch of a Deal Lugger.

The original painting, by Lieut. Henry Wise Harvey RN (circa. 1840), is in Deal Maritime Museum. Note the gateposts of the Naval Dockyard (said still to exist at the entrance to a Kentish farmyard) and the windmill which stood opposite the Naval Hospital. (see page 72) (Print and details kindly provided by Mr Les Cozens.)

"HALT—SMUGGLERS."—PAINTED BY H. P. PARKER.—EXHIBITION OF THE NATIONAL INSTITUTION.

The artist Henry Parker (1795-1873) specialised in depicting the smuggler at work, especially on the Kent coast. (see Rough, Rude Men.)

161

'Jack's Farewell'

Index

Admiralty House, Deal 63, 65
Aldington village 96, 97, 111
Aldington smugglers 22, 112, 113, 114, 128
Army employed against smugglers 30

Basden, William 90
Beachy Head 73, 150, 153
Bexhill 60, 115
'Blues, The' see Aldington smugglers
Broadstairs 73, 76
Brookland affray, The 95, 118
Bushell, James 109, 110
Butcher, Henry 86

Camber 95
Coast Blockade, The:
  development (map) front end papers
  early days 61
  organisation and personnel 75, 152
  Customs report on 79, 150
  expenditure 82
  expansion 83
  friction with Folkestone magistrates 85
  defied by Hastings fishermen 97
  decline accelerates 114
  disbandment 116
  criticism of 116
  defence of 117
  vessels serving in 132
  shore stations listed 135
  in fiction 154
  personnel mentioned: —
      Autridge, — 114, Baker, Francis 79
      Basden, William 89, Brent, Thomas
      89, Carr, Washington 194, Digby,
      Edward 95, 118, 119, Douglas, —
      85, England, George 99, Everett,
      Samuel 105, Finch, Godfrey
      Springall 120, Gardiner, Richard
      77, 118, Graham, — 87, Green,
      John 85, Gruebke, Ephraim 89,
      Hamilton, Thomas 105, 107, 125,
      Hellard, Samuel 89, 108, 111, 122,
      Hunter, Robert 94, James, — 95,
      Jones, Richard 87, Manning, Dennis

41, 77, 125, McCulloch, William
11, 12, 20, 30, 61, 73, 79, 83, 93,
99, 116, 127, 146, 150, McKenzie,
John 95, Miller, Charles 68,
Mingaye, William James 115, 123,
124, 126, Mitchell, William 89,
Morgan, Richard 17, 106, 111,
Newman, — 7, Newton, Charles
James Franklin 95, 124, Nicol,
James 120, Norcott, Patrick 115,
O'Mainnin, Dennis see Manning,
Dennis, Peat, David 71, 94, 95,
Pickett, Michael 106, 111, Pigot,
Hugh 17, 110, 127, 124, Sheahan,
David 85, Snow, Sydenham 103,
Sweeny, Mark 99, Walker, James
85, Walker, John 94, Wooldridge,
Richard 94
  NB Further names are listed on page
  129
Coast Guard 79
Customs Departments — strengths and
salaries 83

Deal 63, 65, 69, 71, 78, 84, 118
  reacts to Blockade 20
  regatta 16

Dover 106, 108, 111
  regatta 16
  steam packet leaving 24
  Castle 42
Dungeness 125, 152
Dymchurch 77, 105

England, George — murder trial 101

Flogging in the Royal Navy 34, 35, 37
Folkestone 79, 95
  Magistrates' attitude to Blockade 85

Haddock, Captain William 28
Hamilton, Midshipman Thomas — ordeal in
  the Dymchurch 'noggin' 105-107

Hart, Mr — (Folkestone JP) 87
Hastings 116
  Fishermen defy the Blockade 95
Hellard, Lieut. Samuel — career 122
  investigates irregularities at Shorncliffe
    91
  reports Morgan's death 108
  tracks down the killers 111
Herne Bay 103
Hobday, Mr — (Folkestone JP) 87
Hythe 74, 85, 109

Land smugglers 15

Manning, Dennis 41, 77
McCulloch, Captain William
  early life 61
  appointed Post-Captain 63
  begins campaign against smugglers 63
  death 64
  assessment of his character 66
  makes his mark 69
  takes over shore stations 73
  service record 145
  genealogy 146
  marriage 149
Margate 104
McKenzie, Midshipman John — killed by
  smugglers 95
Metcalfe, Robert 89

Napoleon's opinion of English smugglers 15
Nelson's attitude to flogging 37
New Bethlem Hospital (RN asylum) 32
Newhaven 60, 124
  church restored with help of the
    Blockade 123
Norcott, Lieut Patrick secures discharge
  from the Blockade 115
North Foreland 153
'North Foreland' inn 86
North Kent smuggling gang smashed 104

O'Mainnin, Dennis see Manning, Dennis

Peat, Lieut David — commended for
  keeness 71
  'a Hard Fighter, of Reckless Courage' 94
Pegwell Bay 159
Port Admiral's residence, Deal — see
  Admiralty House
Poskett, William stands trial for smuggling
  at Folkestone 87
Preventive Waterguard, The 30

Quested, Cephas tried at Old Bailey 97

Ramillies HMS 51
Ransley George (i) 22, 108, 111, 112
Ransley, George (ii) 23
Reculver 83
Renwick, Captain Thomas 61
Riding officers 28, 29
Royal Navy, The:
  life in 31
  insanity rate
  asylum 32
  fatalities (1810) 33
  medical care 38
  Hospital at Greenwich 40
  ships lost 1793-1815 42
  hierarchy 43
  dress 49
  terminology 137
Rye 26, 66, 95, 126, 134

Sandgate 80, 81
Sea smugglers 15
Selsey 93
Selsey Bill 71
Sheerness 60
Shellness 114
Sheppey 68, 71, 79, 83, 150, 153
Ships, the Revd. Burne complaint to
  Capt. McCulloch 93
'Ship Inn', Herne Bay 103
Ships that served in the Blockade (list) 132
Shorncliffe 89, 90, 91
South Foreland 153
Smugglers mentioned in the text:

Bailey, Robert 112, 113, Bailey Samuel
112, Baker, David 104, Brown, Thomas
114, Buffington, John 104, Bushell,
James 109, 110, Carden, Francis 104,
Clements, Joseph 104, Coltrup, Henry
114, Denard, Thomas 112, Fagg, Daniel
104, Gilbert, Joseph 104, Giles, Charles
104, Gill, John 104, Gillian, Thomas
104, Godden, Thomas 85, Gummer,
Stephen 104, Hall, James 104, Keen,
Richard 104, Mace, James 86, Meredith,
John 104, Mount, Thomas 104, Poskett,
William 87, Quested, James 110,
Quested, Cephas 96, 97, 110, Ransley,
George (i) 22, 108, 111, 112, Ransley,
George (ii) 23, Rolfe, James 104, Smith
(Mrs—) 87, Smith Henry 104, Stokes,
Thomas 104, Taylor, James 104, White,
Charles 104, Wilsden, John 104, Wire
(Wyor) Richard 112, 113, Wire (Wyor)
William 112, Wood, Thomas 114,

Woollett, Thomas 104,
Worthington,— 13

Smuggling penalties 21
Smuggling statistics (1723-32) 27
Snow, Midshipman Sydenham, killed by
smugglers 103
South Kent smuggling gang—see Aldington
gang
Swain, John, killed by Blockade seaman 99
Sweeney, Lieut Mark, reports on Hastings
incident 99

Tub sinking 19

Whitstable smugglers 20
Wooldridge, Richard, killed by
smugglers 94
Wraight, Robert, acquitted of smuggling
at Old Bailey 97

NOTES

NOTES

Dunstable
Aylesbury
OXFORD
St. Albans
Watford
Swindon
High Wycombe
Uxbridge
Henley
Windsor
Richmond
Reading
Hungerford
Hampton Court
Kingston
Epsom
Basingstoke
Guildford
Dorking
Reigate
Alton
Horsham
Winchester
Southampton
Petersfield
Southsea
Lymington
Marchwood
Calshot Castle
Beaulieu River
Hamble River
Stokes Bay
Chichester
Arundel
Worthing
Shoreham
BRIGHT
Bognor
Elmer
Littlehampton
Pagham
Selsey
Thorney
Hayling Island
Langston Harbor
Chichester Harbor
Southsea Castle
Milford
Barton Cliff
Yarmouth
East Cowes
Ryde
Bembridge
I. of WIGHT
Brook
Sandown
Ventnor
Atherfield
St. Catherine's Pt.
Bognor
Ryde
South Yarmouth
N E W